Enterprise 2.0
The Art of Letting Go

Enterprise 2.0
The Art of Letting Go

Willms Buhse, Sören Stamer (Eds.)

iUniverse, Inc.
New York Bloomington

Enterprise 2.0 - The Art of Letting Go

Editorial content: Tina Kulow, Lilian Mrusek
Proofreading: Tracy Newton
Translations: Edward Bradburn
Cover design: Hartwig Otto and Carsten Raffel, GUPPY Designerschwarm

iUniverse books may be ordered through booksellers or by contacting:

iUniverse
1663 Liberty Drive
Bloomington, IN 47403
www.iuniverse.com
1-800-Authors (1-800-288-4677)

Because of the dynamic nature of the Internet, any Web addresses or links contained in this book may have changed since publication and may no longer be valid. The views expressed in this work are solely those of the author and do not necessarily reflect the views of the publisher, and the publisher hereby disclaims any responsibility for them.

ISBN: 978-1-4401-0809-9 (pbk)
ISBN: 978-1-4401-0810-5 (ebk)

Library of Congress Control Number: 2008942351

Printed in the United States of America

iUniverse rev. date: 12/9/2008

Table of Contents

Preface

When we broached the idea of a book project to a number of authors at the first Enterprise 2.0 conference in Boston in 2007, the answer we got was: *"Enterprise 2.0 – as a book? Hmm. Interesting idea. Hadn't thought about that"*. And that is precisely the aim of this book: to stimulate interesting and valuable ideas on the subject. We wanted to dedicate an entire book to a subject that had previously been largely confined to discussions within the Internet blogosphere. We wanted to not only reach readers outside this environment, but also stimulate further discussion on Enterprise 2.0. This book therefore aims to bring together leading experts and pioneers in the field, presenting their views as part of a compendium in order to analyze a number of aspects of Enterprise 2.0. We have gone to great lengths to ensure the various contributions retain their original character and intention (despite translation).

At this point, we would like to extend our heartfelt thanks to all authors who have given us insights into their experiences, thoughts, and visions. We have greatly enjoyed working with you all.

This book owes a great deal the many helping hands that have been busy behind the scenes. We would therefore like to thank the following people in particular for their personal commitment, on which this book has depended: Tina Kulow, for supporting both the book and its authors; Lilian Mrusek, for her hard work in communicating with the publishers; Tracy Newton, for her meticulous proof-reading and editing; Hartwig Otto, for the design; Edward Bradburn, for the translations.

Dear Reader, we hope that you will find this book a source of pleasure and inspiration, and we wish you a steady hand in the art of letting go. We look forward to you sharing your experiences, opinions, and ideas by posting at blog.coremedia.com.

Willms Buhse and Sören Stamer

Götz Hamann
Prologue

[handwritten margin note: or just another mechanism to control knowledge workers?]

This book not only presents a strategy for liberation – it is also a plan of attack. Combining their forces, the authors take on one of the central principles of capitalism: the traditional division of work. In their sights is the legacy of two men whose influence can hardly be overestimated. The first is Henry Ford, who popularized assembly line production nearly a hundred years ago; the second is Frederick Taylor, who developed the theory that there is only ever one "best method" applicable to a specific task. Taken together – assembly line and rationalized workflow – these two factors form the essence of the traditional division of work, and even today they influence the organization of almost every company in existence. Without them, the triumph of capitalism and the familiar high standard of living in our Western industrialized nations would be unimaginable. And that's not the end of it. We turn to Asia and see that they are now reliving what the West experienced fifty years ago.

Yet the principles that once brought the West such power are fast becoming a damper on the economy, argue the authors in this book. The Internet pioneer Andrew McAfee, the corporate advisor Don Tapscott, the entrepreneur Sören Stamer, and many others make the following claim: the traditional division of work is in many cases a hindrance to the workforce. They name their alternative strategy "Enterprise 2.0."

[handwritten margin note: Agile?]

— really?!

Those who challenge a principle as successful as the traditional division of work must of course produce convincing arguments – and that is unquestionably the case here. Fordian and Taylorist ideals have been slowly losing their relevance for day-to-day business for a while now, and this is by no means only applicable to the Internet economy. Even in traditional sectors such as mechanical engineering, complex service provision constitutes a large and increasingly significant proportion of the total value chain both before, during, and after the actual production of a piece of machinery. Precisely-defined workflows, hierarchies, and workplace specialization are losing significance as a natural result of these developments. The difference is between the assembly line workers of yesteryear and the modern employees who – across the entire globe – are busy constructing and maintaining machinery, writing the necessary software for it, and modifying units to fit into a complex manufacturing process. Supported by the Internet and mobile networks, staff communication and knowledge as well as their personal networks are becoming increasingly central factors for business.

? really?

This book reviews the undeveloped potential for transformation and growth that lies dormant in the business world. In the process, this book foregoes an analysis of the cost of change, concentrating instead on the clear and unambiguous value of the idea in knowledge-intensive industries, where it can revolutionize a company's ability to exploit the knowledge possessed by its employees – and even motivate them to achieve maximal creativity and productivity.

Google or Microsoft? Deutsche Bank or Citigroup? The first skirmish was won by the company whose managers were the first to appreciate that search was the core Internet service, and which was then subsequently able to attract the best developers in order to maintain and even expand on its initial advantage. That was Google. It still is Google.

And Google it will remain for a long while to come. That fact is demonstrated by growth of earnings, the ROI for Internet business, and the global market share of online advertising. Knowledge, communication, the networks that they create, and a company infrastructure that maximizes their use are more important than ever. This was also the case with Deutsche Bank. A combination of particularly far-sighted staff and appropriate processes within the company enabled the bank to make accurate assessments of the growing risk within the US property markets. Looking back, says CEO Joseph Ackermann, the decision was made with only a small majority. Yet the decision was still made – granting the bank a number of months to decrease its risk involvement. The US-owned Citigroup, on the other hand, was steamrollered by the crisis, had to resort to writing off several billions of dollars in losses, and needed to be stabilized with capital provided by a sovereign wealth fund from Abu Dhabi.

In 2004, the journalist James Surowiecki wrote in his book "The Wisdom of Crowds": „Corporate strategy is all about collecting information from many different sources, evaluating the probabilities of potential outcomes, and making decisions in the face of an uncertain future." In recent years, the managers of Google and Deutsche Bank have proven themselves to be highly capable strategists. Yet how can one do the same?

If knowledge worker productivity is the factor that makes the difference, how can this productivity be increased? How should a company be organized to convert workforce knowledge into profit in a way that is superior to the competition in terms of both speed and quality? The message of this book is clear: turn your back on the theories of Ford and Taylor and embrace an entirely new principle. The principle in question is termed Enterprise 2.0 and is introduced in the first chapter by the Internet pioneer Andrew McAfee ("A Definition of Enterprise 2.0").

Enterprise 2.0 attempts to utilize the creative power of the workforce comprehensively. To achieve this, it offers employees the opportunity to take on responsibilities beyond those of a narrowly-defined job description, to express opinions, and to let themselves be influenced by individual aptitude to a greater extent in their daily business work. The ideal is to have as many stakeholders as possible in free collaboration, unfettered by constraints stemming from organizational structure, processes, or technology. The entrepreneur Sören Stamer considers the practical side of this, discussing how some boundaries must be crossed and others respected. He himself initiated and managed such a process at CoreMedia, the software company he co-founded ("Enterprise 2.0 – Learning by Doing").

Everything and anything that fosters or improves human social behavior, or uses it to generate added value, is encouraged. Writing in "Winning with Enterprise 2.0," the corporate advisor Don Tapscott even calls this the "Age of Collaboration." In order to attain the greatest possible level of information transfer, Tapscott utilizes a kind of software that has now come to be referred to generally as "social software": wikis, instant messaging, and blogs, plus software for social bookmarking and social networking.

An intentional effect of Enterprise 2.0 is the loss of control in its traditionally-recognized form. Time recording, departmental boundaries, narrowly-defined task areas, and the splitting of larger corporations into a multitude of subsidiaries all have a fairly dramatic and negative effect on the network effects obtained via Enterprise 2.0. Those on the other hand who wish to network their workforce as comprehensively as possible must recognize that information no longer flows in the long-accepted channels from top to bottom (or vice versa), manipulated by many filters on its way, but instead, simply spreads unhindered in all directions at once. Knowledge becomes shared and is not used primarily for maintaining one's own power base. In such an environment, the individual manager will find it far harder to manipulate information for his or her own personal benefit. This thesis is conclusively argued for by David Weinberger, a Fellow of the Berkman Center for Internet and Society at Harvard University ("The Risk of Control"). Both the company and its IT architecture must accommodate and foster a participative culture. Both Tapscott and Stamer argue that this results in the formation of topic- and product-oriented teams that transcend traditional departmental boundaries. Ideally, the team-building process is either partially or entirely self-organized.

And this process of change is not confined to businesses: it has long since reached their customers, too. These customers no longer have to rely on what the company itself tells them about its products and services on offer. Forums, newsgroups, blogs, and other sources of information have established themselves online. Unavoidably, those in the business of running a company must now engage in dialogue with their customers. In "Beauty Comes from Within: The New Culture of Communication in Enterprise 2.0," Willms Buhse, Marketing Director at CoreMedia, discusses the ways in which marketing can face up to these changed rules of play, and how taking a different approach to dialog with customers can also effect changes within the company itself.

The goal of this strategy is clear: achieving increased productivity from knowledge workers. The crucial role played by sustained communication between stakeholders and established business networks was argued for by the American organizational theorist Mark Granovetter as early as 1973 and his theory remains highly influential to this day. Granovetter's publication of the time was an article entitled "The Strength of Weak Ties." He argued that companies should not stop at simply doing everything in their power to ensure that knowledge workers can work well and efficiently with their trusted colleagues. It is also insufficient to simply put together a team that explicitly unites a broad spectrum of talents and subject skills.

Granovetter argued that companies will not reap the biggest benefits just by intensifying the close ('strong') work relationships already in existence. At least the same investment should also be made to foster 'weak' relationships. These, he argued, can prove to be of critical importance for the future development of a business. These weak ties are defined by Granovetter as casual contacts. His argument is that a person who tends to interact chiefly within a group of trusted individuals (and where this group itself focuses strongly on its own concerns) has a low rate of exposure to new ideas. Casual contacts on the other hand, argues Granovetter, have the advantage that they provide a means of accessing a pool of previously untapped knowledge in a comparatively quick and simple fashion, and the results are also multiplied by network effects. Casual contacts can thus serve as good sources of information and significantly increase the rate of innovation within a business.

That summarizes, one could say, the theoretical point of origin for Enterprise 2.0. Considered in this light, the chances are especially favorable for Enterprise 2.0 to achieve the greatest competitive knowledge advantage: it fosters internal communication, emphasizes the unhindered flow of information, and encourages as many employees as possible to think outside their old job descriptions and participate creatively in the company's business. Computers, the Internet, and 'social software' constitute the ideal tools for this process, since these are – taken together – more effective than anything available even a few years ago.

While most definitely a guide for entrepreneurs, helping them help their knowledge workers to deliver excellent results, this book also showcases a number of articles that are quite utopian in their consideration of society and the economy. These articles consider Enterprise 2.0 to be the ideal company form for people in general. They promise us a world in which each individual is – and is held to be – largely responsible for his or her own career and journey through life. Everyone must make a conscious contribution to his or her own job security. While restrictions are relaxed to foster personal well-being, the attendant freedom must be used to ensure growth for all – to remain competitive within the knowledge and network economy. Ultimately, a process of self-actualization – spurred on by entrepreneurial activity – occurs both at work and in one's personal life, whereby the two become intermingled.

Such theorizations represent a watershed in the history of Western sociological and economic thought. Grossly simplified, the capitalism of the Manchester school still swallowed the individual whole, only to discard that person once his or her usefulness was exhausted. In contrast, the industries of the 20th century expended a good deal of effort on maintaining and qualifying the employee's capability for work, and offering the workforce increased security via the services and safety nets of the welfare state. Yet for the individual working in such newly-bureaucratized companies, limited to performing a narrowly-defined task set, there was little room for personal responsibility or development. The greater security came at a price.

In the work of authors such as Don Tapscott, one finds that the contemporary knowledge worker views this traditional business environment as an unnecessary tyranny. In comparison, the contemporary network economy, together with start-ups and highly-skilled service providers, offers its individual employees more freedom of action than ever. And this freedom is granted in the firm conviction that many people are able and willing to contribute greater value to their business than is permitted by a traditional company structure.

Enterprise 2.0 naturally has its predecessors in the world at large – although one finds them far removed from Internet business. An overview of these forerunners is given by Michael Koch ("Lessons from the Past: Computer-Supported Collaborative Work & Co."). Computer-supported teamwork has been in existence for twenty years and group work in automobile manufacturing is legendary. Investment bankers work in teams, while developers in large corporations – scattered around the globe and over multiple time zones – work on the same project, staying connected via the company-internal computer systems. Nonetheless, those who survey the organizational make-up of the average global corporation or the typical, tightly-structured mid-size company will conclude that the legacy of Ford and Taylor is still very much alive: Sales, Marketing, Development, Production, Payroll, Administration, IT – and, of course, the Executive. The corporate pigeon-holing system does not expect its employees to move between 'boxes' once they have been categorized. While it is true that many managers have realized just how unproductive this often turns out to be, they persist in refusing to change the organizational structure.

They have their reasons. At least one of these reasons is solid, although it is not considered in this book: change comes at a cost. Not everyone is able or willing to act as an entrepreneur – not everyone has a creative streak that lends itself to new product development. Some employees will not improve once the dependable structures of their workplace are removed and some will be incapable of regulating their own workload. Successful companies must also offer these kinds of employees an environment in which they can be maximally productive. In addition, major corporations must master the difficult balancing act resulting from interdepartmental collaboration. Time proves to be a scarce resource, meaning that someone somewhere must still take responsibility for deciding how staff will spend this precious commodity. What is creative? What is a waste of time? Not everyone will succeed in the day-to-day management of an Enterprise 2.0.

Beyond that, there are reasons that, although important in themselves, also underscore the need for a book such as this one and, at the same time, speak volumes about today's managers. The traditional division of work still counts as the surest way to exercise power and the most effective means by which one can control an organization. In her chapter "Reality Check Enterprise 2.0: The State of Play Within German Companies," Nicole Dufft from Berlecon Research provides us with clear evidence that ignorance of the Enterprise 2.0 principles addressed in this book is still par for the course. Her research shows us that half of the managers from knowledge-intensive industries that participated in her survey are either unfamiliar with the term "Web 2.0" or, if aware of the term, consider it to be a mere media buzzword. Companies employing managers such as these are assuredly many years away from being able to apply the ideas of Enterprise 2.0.

In considering the consequences of the ITC revolution of the past few decades, while suggesting new approaches to the handling of real-world applications, this book forms part of a long tradition. This discourse begins with an essay by Herbert A. Simon (subsequently awarded the Nobel Prize for Business) entitled "Designing Organizations for an Information-Rich World." Writing in the late 1960s, Simon considered how the world of information and knowledge management would be likely to change during the looming computer age. He was followed, some thirty years later, by the visionaries of the Internet age – including Nicholas Negroponte from MIT ("Being Digital"), the digital commentator and digerati member Esther Dyson ("Release 2.0: A Design for Living in the Digital Age") and Don Tapscott. It was Tapscott who more than a decade ago realized the true dimension of the changes to which companies might be subjected ("The Digital Economy. Promise and Peril in the Age of Networked Intelligence"). Others, such as Kevin Kelly, journalist for *Wired* magazine, saw a power in the New Economy that would forever change the rules by which we do business ("New Rules for the New Economy"). Alterations in lifestyle and the workplace, technical innovation, and thousands of start-ups would all act to sweep away the major corporations. Nevertheless, Kelly chose to ignore a number of inconvenient facts: first, most households ten years ago did not possess anything like sufficient access to computers and the Internet; second (and consequently) this rendered impractical a great many business ideas; third, the New Economy, for all its semi-religious hyperbole, failed to deliver a sound blueprint for the day-to-day business environment of workers in the knowledge economy. However, only a short while after the bubble burst in 2001, authors began seeking out the innovations that had weathered the storm, referring to them collectively as the "Next Economy," for example (title of a work by the journalist Thomas Fischermann). All these considerations lead directly to Enterprise 2.0.

Now is therefore the time to set the market straight. Handsome rewards are in store for those who create an organizational structure that increases the productivity in this knowledge economy. And this book undoubtedly provides much stimulus to do so.

WORKS CITED

Granovetter, Mark (1973): The Strength of Weak Ties. In: American Journal of Sociology, 78 (May): 1360-1380. Available from JSTOR's online database at: http://tinyurl.com/2s9gck.

Simon, Herbert A. (1996): Designing Organizations for an Information–Rich World. In: Lamberton, Donald M. (Ed.): The Economics of Communication and Information, Cheltenham/Brookefield, pp. 187-202.

Negroponte, Nicholas (1995): Being Digital. Knopf.

Dyson, Esther (1997): Release 2.0: A Design for Living in the Digital Age. Broadway Books.

Tapscott, Don (1996): The Digital Economy: Promise and Peril in the Age of Networked Intelligence. McGraw-Hill, New York. Summarized at: http://tinyurl.com/29wojy.

Kelly, Kevin (1996), New Rules for the New Economy, Viking. Online version at http://www.kk.org/newrules/.

Andrew McAfee
A Definition of Enterprise 2.0

Enterprise 2.0 is the use of emergent social software platforms within companies, or between companies and their partners or customers. Platforms are digital environments in which contributions and interactions are globally visible and persistent over time, not channels (like e-mail) where transmissions can't be easily traced or consulted. Social software enables people to rendezvous, connect, or collaborate through computer-mediated[1] communication and to form online communities[2]. The software is emergent, which means that it is freeform, and that it contains mechanisms to let the patterns and structure inherent in people's interactions become visible over time. Enterprise 2.0 is lightweight: it is not hard to deploy or learn. The software is initially unstructured, free of up-front workflow, and is eventually emergent and self-organizing. It is egalitarian, or indifferent to formal organizational identities, and accepting of many types of data. Enterprise 2.0 is a decent vehicle for capturing or pointing to knowledge. In other words, it might fulfill some of the promise of knowledge management systems. The success of Enterprise 2.0 is largely dependent on human issues, not technical ones.

The state of the meme

Enterprise 2.0 technologies don't respect existing horizontal and vertical boundaries within organizations. These tools don't care much who you are or where you fit in the org chart. In their pure form they accept contributions regardless of source and display them regardless of audience. Many have pointed out that this is likely to make lots of people uncomfortable. As Max Weber wrote over 80 years ago, „Every bureaucracy seeks to increase the superiority of the professionally informed by keeping their knowledge and intentions secret...Bureaucracy naturally welcomes a poorly informed and hence a powerless parliament— at least in so far as ignorance somehow agrees with the bureaucracy's interests."[3] Knowledge and intentions both become more widely visible with Enterprise 2.0.

CEOs, CIOs, and users welcome this development. I've given Enterprise 2.0 talks here at Harvard Business School to participants in our most senior executive education program, to owners and founders of their own small and medium-sized companies, to IT/IS managers, and to alumni. Reactions from all these groups have been highly positive. One of the owner/founders stopped my spiel, looked around the room, and said to his colleagues something close to „Hey everyone, if we trust our employees, and if we really do believe that they're out most important asset, and if we think that we have a healthy corporate culture, then we have to do this stuff." Lots of other postings I've read make the same point —that top managers and technologists want to deploy these tools.

Some middle managers don't. Weber's quote probably applies most strongly to the population of middle managers who are used to acting as the main conduit for information into and especially out of their groups. Prior to the network era, these folk could exercise pretty effective control over how the ‚rest of the world' perceived their groups by filtering and selectively presenting information.

Enterprise IT, like enterprise resource planning (ERP), reduced the ability of middle managers to control the flow of structured transactional information (how much inventory do we have?, how many orders did we ship last month?, how long did it take us to get paid?, etc.).

Enterprise 2.0 technologies threaten to do the same for unstructured knowledge-based information. These technologies bring new architectures of participation. As Mitch Kapor brilliantly said, „Architecture is politics."[4] And Ross Mayfield pointed out that Enterprise 2.0 overturns previously encoded political bargains.[5]

Simpler is better. A very thoughtful e-mail I got from reader TR made a great point: „Wikis/blogs, etc. are effective because they're simple and people can get things done quickly. I know this is a simple point, and I know you've made it (when describing wikis), but what if this point overwhelms all the others in significance?" Indeed, what if? I love writing about highfalutin concepts like emergence, but it's important to not lose sight of the fact that people use these tools because they work for them, and they work in large part because they're so easy to use. We should all tape to our walls wiki inventor Ward Cunningham's driving question: „What's the simplest thing that could possibly work?" Doing so might help us overcome our innate desire to use technology to impose structure, and also help companies deliver IT more cheaply. Enterprise 2.0, in other words, is about new communities, not communities' new plumbing. If we keep talking about the plumbing we're going to lose the attention of business leaders. And that would be a shame.

It's not not about the technology

One of the most common phrases I hear in discussions of *any* type of IT initiative, from Enterprise 2.0 to ERP to systems integration, is „It's not about the technology (INATT)." I've heard this from vendors, consultants, technologists, executives inside and outside the IT function, analysts, pundits, and academics. Searching for the exact phrase yields about 1,800 results on Google Blog Search, 17,700 on Google Web Search, and at least one book title. I'm sure I've said it myself a few times, although I try not to.

People usually mean one of two things when they say INATT; one of them is correct but somewhat uninformative, and the other conveys a lot of information, but is incorrect and even dangerous. The correct-but-bland meaning is „It's not about the technology *alone*." In other words, a piece of technology will not spontaneously or independently start delivering value, generating benefits, and doing precisely what its deployers want it to do. Technologies have to be managed in order to do any of these things; they're not magic bullets or miracle cures.

This version of INATT is clearly accurate, but how often, and to whom, does it need to be said? I very rarely come across anyone these days who thinks that technologies *are* magic bullets. All the companies I work with know from ample experience that IT efforts need to be managed. They may not handle their deployments perfectly, but they're well past the stage of setting out a new piece of IT, then sitting back and waiting for the benefits to accrue. This version of INATT might be a useful reminder to managers who are underestimating the amount of change management required to succeed on a given project, but it's not really news to them.

The other meaning behind INATT is „The details of this technology can be ignored for the purposes of this discussion." If true, this is great news for every generalist, because it means that they don't need to take time to familiarize themselves with any aspect of the technology in question. They can just treat it as a black box that will convert specified inputs into specified outputs if installed correctly.

This perspective is dangerous because it essentially denies two important facts: that technologies can differ from each other in salient ways, and that they can change over time. Losing sight of either of these can lead to confusion, or worse. For example, it's well established that IT can help integrate the enterprise, but do they all do so in the same way? INATT, taken to the extreme, would cause a company to treat IM and R/3 the same way (after all, they both integrate the enterprise and enable business processes). A lot of my work, for example these articles,[6] is an attempt to articulate the managerially relevant differences across technologies (McAfee 2005). The second version of INATT encourages listeners not to keep such differences in mind, and I think that's the wrong idea.

INATT, version 2, also encourages the view that there's nothing new under the sun – that one generation of technology aimed at addressing a business problem is the same as all other generations. So (for example) we need to collaborate and share knowledge better, but it's not about the technology. We've been disappointed with our past results in these areas for reasons that have nothing to do with the technologies we were using, and there's nothing about any new technologies that gives us better chances of success now.

This sense of INATT is pessimistic and self-defeating, even if it's not intended to be. It denies that there can be improvements, incremental or radical, in the ability of technologies to accomplish important goals. I disagree categorically with this. A lot of my writing on Enterprise 2.0, in my blog and elsewhere, has stressed that the IT toolkit available to help with collaboration, innovation, and knowledge sharing has recently become a great deal richer and better. INATT works against my goals in this area, and I've started to cringe when I hear it.

Social Networking Software (SNS) and its direct applicability within companies

When I talk about Enterprise 2.0, the most common question I hear is some variant of „How do we convince our colleagues (or bosses) of the value of deploying these technologies?" I've usually replied by describing the capabilities brought by Enterprise 2.0 – new modes of collaboration, giving people an opportunity to express their judgment, and self-organization – and by repeating my aversion to quantitative IT business cases containing rosy ROI or NPV figures. I've also stressed that we need to keep amassing case studies to demonstrate what's possible. I often get the impression, though, that this answer leaves some people unsatisfied.

I've recently been hearing a more focused version of this question. My presentations on Enterprise 2.0 now always include a discussion of social networking software (SNS) like Facebook and its direct applicability within companies. SNS lets users build a network of friends, keep abreast of what that network is up to, and even exploit it by doing things like posting a question that all friends will see. All of these activities, especially the latter two, seem like they'd be highly valuable within a company, especially a large and/or geographically distributed one where you can't access all colleagues just by bumping into them in the hallway.

Even after describing the benefits of SNS this way, though, I almost always get a question like „But how do I convince my company that an internal Facebook is a good idea and a tool that will enhance productivity? Most of our executives still look at it as nothing but a time waster – a tool for planning happy hour and online popularity contests."

I came across an elegant and convincing answer to this question when I remembered one of the readings I did as a doctoral student. Perhaps the best thing about HBS's DBA program when I went through it a decade ago was that students spent much of their first year immersed in many literatures relevant to business study (sociology, organizational psychology, economics, etc.) rather than immediately diving into only one. This approach exposed us to many powerful ideas and thinkers, and forever put the lie to the idea that there's one best way of looking at organizational issues, or one academic discipline that contains all the insights.

We read a fair bit written by Mark Granovetter, a sociologist now at Stanford, who must be one of the most frequently referenced of all organizational scholars. In 1973, Granovetter wrote „The Strength of Weak Ties" (SWT), a seminal article that's been cited a jaw-dropping 5,111 times according to Google Scholar.

Companies that rely heavily on innovation have always spent a great deal of time, money, and effort on ways to help knowledge workers interact better with their close colleagues. These companies obsess about office and lab layouts, trying to ensure that people flow past each other often and feel drawn to common work areas. They assemble cross-functional teams and try to make sure that these groups have enough of the right kinds of diversity (whatever that is). They hold brainstorming sessions and off-sites where coworkers can interact with the same set of colleagues, but differently.

Granovetter's great insight in SWT and later work was that these activities help strengthen already strong ties, but that weak ties might actually be the more important ones for innovation and knowledge sharing. Strong ties and weak ties are exactly what they sound like. Strong ties between people arise from long-term, frequent, and sustained interactions; weak ties from infrequent and more casual ones. The 'problem' with strong ties is that if persons A and B have a strong tie, they're also likely to be strongly tied to all members of each other's networks. In other words, there's likely to be a lot of overlap in their friendship circles.

This might be a good thing in many ways, but it's bad news if A needs a piece of knowledge that she can't find inside her own friendship circle. Because of the overlap, B's circle is likely to be redundant with A's, and so unhelpful to her. In other words, her tie to B does her little good in her search for knowledge. If A and C have a weak tie, however, many of C's friends are likely to be strangers to A, and so are good resources as she looks to inform herself.

A tidy summary of SWT's conclusion is that strong ties are unlikely to be bridges between networks, while weak ties are good bridges. Bridges help solve problems, gather information, and import unfamiliar ideas. They help get work done quicker and better. The ideal network for a knowledge worker probably consists of a core of strong ties and a large periphery of weak ones. Because weak ties by definition don't require a lot of effort to maintain, there's no reason not to form a lot of them (as long as they don't come at the expense of strong ties).

Subsequent research has explored whether Granovetter's hypotheses and conclusions apply within companies, and they appear to be quite robust. My former HBS colleague Morton Hansen, for example, found that weak ties helped product development groups accomplish projects faster. Hansen, Marie Louise Mors, and Bjorn Lovas further showed that weak ties helped by reducing information search costs. And Daniel Levin and Rob Cross found that the benefits of weak ties were amplified if knowledge seekers trusted that information sources were competent in their fields.

The implication for SNS is obvious: Facebook and its peers should be highly valuable for businesses because they're tools for increasing the density of weak ties within a company, as well as outside it. My

Facebook friends are a large group of people from diverse backgrounds who have very little in common with each other. Furthermore, their profiles give me a decent way to evaluate their expertise. These online friends, in other words, are a large group of bridges to other networks. Facebook already provides me a few good ways to activate these bridges for my own purposes. I anticipate that enterprise SNS (whatever that turns out to be) will have many more. One experiment to watch in this area is A-space, an SNS established by the US Directorate of National Intelligence.

I also think that employees who blog behind the firewall are establishing something like weak ties with all of their colleagues. If a decent search exists, any employee can find out if their blogging peers have sought-after knowledge or expertise. The ties in this instance are potential rather than actual, but they're still valuable in the way that all options are.

In fact, the concept of an option is a useful one for understanding the overall power of weak ties. An employee's strong ties give her colleagues. Her weak ones open up options. Technologies that help weak ties proliferate therefore also provide options. Given how cheap they are, and how many options they bring, they seem like one of the best investments out there.

How to hit the Enterprise 2.0 bull's-eye

My colleague Clay Christensen[7] stresses that managers are voracious consumers of theory. In other words, they value ways to think about their world and mental tools that will let them make decisions and predictions with a level of confidence higher than they get from experience and intuition alone.

I've been reminded of Clay's insight because I've recently had some success using a longstanding theory to explain to executives the value of social networking software (SNS) like Facebook. Mark Granovetter's theory of the ‚strength of weak ties' provides a great way to conceptualize the value of SNS. These technologies increase a knowledge worker's number of weak ties (and hence access to non-redundant information and bridges to other networks), and also provide an easy and convenient way to exploit these ties from within the tool itself.

But the intersection of ties and Enterprise 2.0 technologies goes much farther than this. In fact, ties provide a great base for understanding the benefits provided by many Enterprise 2.0 technologies, and for understanding when each one should be deployed. Thinking in terms of ties, in other words, let managers select from among the grab bag of available technologies and also anticipate the benefits they'll get after successful deployment.

Consider the prototypical knowledge worker inside a large, geographically distributed organization (all of what follows also applies for smaller and more centralized organizations, but probably to a lesser extent). She has a relatively small group of close collaborators; these are people with whom she has strong professional ties. Beyond this group, there's also a set that includes people she worked with on a project with in the past, coworkers she interacts with periodically, colleagues she knows via an introduction, and the many other varieties of ,professional acquaintance.' In Granovetter's language, she has weak ties to these people.

Beyond *this* group there's a still-larger set of fellow employees who could be valuable to our prototypical knowledge worker *if only she knew about them.* These are people who could keep her from re-inventing the wheel, answer one of her pressing questions, point her to exactly the right resource, tell her about a really good vendor, consultant, or other external partner, let her know that they were working on a similar problem and had made some encouraging progress, or do any of the other scores of good things that come from a well-functioning tie. By the same token, if our focal worker is a person of good will, there are many other people in the company she could help if her existence, work experiences, and abilities were more widely known.

Of course, there's also a large group in the organization who are just not going to be of much use to our prototypical worker, and vice versa. These people will not form ties. They're simply coworkers, not actual or potential colleagues. It seems at first glance as if it wouldn't be valuable to use any type of technology to bring these people together. This, however, is too hasty a conclusion, as I'll discuss.

The bull's-eye figure below is an extremely simple and not-to-scale representation of the relative size of these groups, from the perspective of our focal knowledge worker. The small core of people with whom she has strong ties is at the center, surrounded by her larger group of weakly-tied colleagues. Potential ties are in the next ring, and coworkers – people with whom valuable ties do not and will not exist – make up the outermost ring. My intuition is that for most knowledge workers the four circles in the figure are nested accurately – that the number of potential ties, for example, is greater than the number of weak ties – even if their relative sizes are way off.

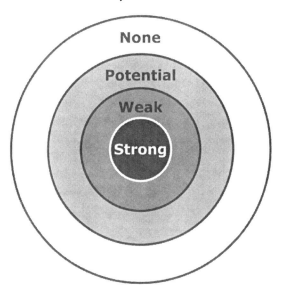

Figure 1: Relative amounts of different types of ties for a prototypical knowledge worker

What does all this have to do with the emergent social software platforms of Enterprise 2.0? Well, there are several such platforms, each of which is valuable in a different way. Wikis, a blogosphere, social networking software, and prediction markets all facilitate Enterprise 2.0

as I've defined it, but they're clearly not identical technologies, or even closely similar ones.

But *how* are they different? Do they do dissimilar things for companies, and to them? And when is each the ‚right answer‘? Answers to these questions arise from the realization that a knowledge worker will want to use a different Enterprise 2.0 technology at each ring in the bull's-eye.

A wiki is the classic Enterprise 2.0 technology for a core of strongly tied knowledge workers who are collaborating on a deliverable. They can use it to generate documents, to debate their contents and structure, track project status, link to other resources, etc. Google Docs and Spreadsheets, Zoho, and other online office productivity suites are similar to wikis in that they allow egalitarian editing of documents, spreadsheets, and presentations by all group members; they're just not currently as extensible as a full wiki.

Evidence suggests that wikis let strongly-tied collaborators get their work done better, faster, and with more agility than was previous possible. With a wiki, what's emergent is the document itself, with ‚document‘ defined broadly. As I wrote earlier, enterprise social networking software lets our prototypical knowledge worker stay in touch with a large network of colleagues, allowing her to keep up to date with that they're doing, working on, and producing. It also lets her tell this network what she's up to.

This might sound like an only marginally useful exercise, but it can in fact be quite powerful because it's a quick and easy way to form connections and make associations that might not ever occur otherwise. I saw this firsthand a couple days ago when one of my Facebook friends told his network via his status message that he was going to accompany a foreign head of state to a high-level meeting on technology issues. Because I was only weakly tied to this person I had no idea that he was that well connected or interested in public policy. But as a result of his Facebook update, which took him about ten seconds to type and me one second to read, I now know who to reach out to should I ever want to dive into European IT issues, or desire an invitation to the Elysée

Palace. SNS lets its users build bridges to new human networks, and lets non-redundant information emerge.

Facebook currently lets members ask their network a question, then collects their answers on one globally-visible page. I imagine that successful enterprise Facebook equivalents will have much more advanced tools to allow members to actively exploit their networks by asking them for assistance, pumping them for information, etc. I also imagine that they'll let users post answers to their most frequently-asked questions, then simply point seekers to this resource. The facts that Facebook has opened its platform to outside applications, and that a consortium of social media providers anchored by Google and MySpace has just announced a common specification for developers, will no doubt hasten the arrival of robust enterprise SNS.

And what about all the people in the third ring of the circle in the figure – the potentially valuable colleagues our knowledge worker just hasn't met yet? Wikis and SNS in their current configurations don't help her learn of the existence of such people, but an internal corporate blogosphere could. Imagine a large company in which most workgroups (divisions, labs, departments, project teams, etc.) blogged, as did many individuals. No one would have time to read all the resulting blogs, of course, and most employees would probably read few of them regularly. But I imagine lots of people would set up searches for words, phrases, or topics of interest (as is possible with Bloglines, Google blog search, and other tools), then check in frequently to see what recent posts show up in their search results. This is the main way that I keep up with the latest writing on „Enterprise 2.0.“ Even articles in print publications get discussed almost immediately in the blogosphere, so I learn about them, too.

I've seen a few surveys indicating that blogs are currently one of the least popular Enterprise 2.0 technologies among CIOs and other decision makers, probably because the business value of internal blogging isn't always clear. Maintaining a blog can seem like shouting into a void, and we all certainly have better things to do than that. The benefit of blogs becomes much clearer when they're seen as tools to convert *potential* ties, strong or weak, into *actual* ones. Prior to the Web 2.0 era I don't believe that good technologies existed to help with this conversion, and the overall toolkit for making employees aware of potentially valuable ties – including newsletters, ‚science fairs,‘ seminar series, etc. – was pretty small. A lively internal blogosphere that includes good search and notification mechanisms represents a significant addition to this toolkit, and can allow productive ties and teams to emerge over time.

The outermost ring of the bull‘s-eye seems like the least amenable to technology – how can the new crop of digital tools productively inter-connect people who really don‘t have anything to say to contribute to each other? Prediction markets do exactly this. Prediction markets are very much like stock markets. They contain securities, each of which has a price. People use the market to trade with each other by buying and selling these securities. Because traders have differing beliefs about what the securities are worth, and because events that occur over time alter these beliefs, the prices of securities also vary over time.

In a stock market like the New York Stock Exchange, the securities being traded are shares in companies, the price of which reflects beliefs about the value of the company. In a corporate prediction market, in contrast, the securities being traded are related to future events such as: „How many units of this product will we sell next quarter?“ „What will our market share be at the end of the quarter?“ „Will our competitor release their product on time?“ „Will we release *our* product on time?“ Such markets can be designed so that security prices are the same as the estimated probability that the event will occur, according to the markets' traders.

Prediction markets provide benefits to the traders in the form of ego boosts and monetary rewards (if a company decides to reward suc-cessful trading that way), and they bring substantial benefits to sponso-ring companies by providing accurate and decisive answers to impor-tant questions. As James Surowiecki wrote in *The Wisdom of Crowds*, „Corporate strategy is all about collecting information from many dif-ferent sources, evaluating the probabilities of potential outcomes, and making decisions in the face of an uncertain future. These are tasks for which [prediction] markets are tailor-made.“

The participants in a prediction market don't have to have any dealings with each other beyond their trades, and often don't even know who they're trading with. So these markets aren't tools to help human networks coalesce; they're just ways to have answers emerge from the self-interested, profit-maximizing activities of a population of traders.

The table below summarizes the potential benefits, candidate technologies, and type of emergence at each ring of the bull's-eye (in other words, for each type of tie). Like the bull's-eye figure itself, it is a drastic simplification of a large and complex set of phenomena. In particular, the entries in the three rightmost columns of the table aren't meant to be mutually exclusive or collectively exhaustive. They simply highlight some important differences at each of the four levels.

Tie Strength	Potential Benefits	Technology Example	What is Emergent?
Strong	Collaboration, Productivity, Agility	Wiki	Document
Weak	Innovation, Non-redundant information, Network bridging	Social Networking Software	Information
Potential	Efficient search, Tie formation	Blogosphere	Team
None	Collective intelligence	Prediction Market	Answer

Figure 2: Potential benefits, candidate technologies and type of emergence within the bull's-eye

I'm hearing from a lot of people that late 2007 is much like late 1997, when technology specialists were getting asked by senior executives „What is the Internet, exactly, why is it a big deal, and what's our Internet strategy?" The question now is „What's Web 2.0 / Enterprise 2.0 / social media, exactly, why is it a big deal, and what's our Web 2.0 / Enterprise 2.0 / social media strategy?" The table, bull's-eye figure, and arguments presented here can help frame discussions around these questions by encouraging decision makers to first focus on what ring(s) of the bull's-eye they're most interested in targeting. Lots of subsequent decisions and activities flow from the answer to this question and from applying a bit of well-established theory (the theory of strong and weak ties) to technology considerations.

WORKS CITED:

Granovetter, Mark (1973): The Strength of Weak Ties. In: American Journal of Sociology, 78, pp. 1360-1380.

Hansen, Morton T. (1999): The Search-Transfer Problem: The Role of Weak Ties in Sharing Knowledge across Organization Subunits. Administrative Science Quarterly, 44 (1), pp. 82-85.

Hansen, Morton T.; Mors, Marie-Luise; Lovas, Bjorn (2005): Knowledge Sharing in Organizations: Multiple Networks, Multiple Phases. In: The Academy of Management Journal, 48 (5), pp. 776-793.

Levin, Daniel Z.; Cross, Rob (2004): The Strength of Weak Ties You Can Trust: The Meditating Role of Trust in Effective Knowledge Transfer. In: Management Science, 50 (11), pp. 1477-1490.

McAfee, Andrew (2003): When Too Much IT Knowledge Is a Dangerous Thing. In: MIT Sloan Management Review, 44 (4), pp. 83-89. http://sloanreview.mit.edu/smr/issue/2003/winter/11//.

Surowiecki, James (2004): The Wisdom of Crowds. Why the Many Are Smarter Than the Few and How Collective Wisdom Shapes Business, economies, Societies and Nations, New York.

Weber, Max (1985): Wirtschaft und Gesellschaft, Tübingen 1922.

Michael Koch
Lessons from the Past – Computer-Supported Collaborative Work & Co.

Introduction

The available literature on social software and Enterprise 2.0 may give some readers the impression that this development is something of a novelty. Observing that no more than five years have passed since the Web 2.0 developments cited as providing the foundation for social software, social software (and thus Enterprise 2.0) is itself assumed to be no more than a few years old. This assumption is both correct and erroneous.

While the term 'social software' has achieved popularity only in the last few years, the core principles of social software and Enterprise 2.0 in particular – i.e., those that support collaboration within the company – are considerably older. Originating with the "Memex" theories of Vannevar Bush in 1945, these were followed by groupware and computer-supported collaborative work (CSCW) in the period from 1970 to the end of the 1990s. Christopher Allen has documented this development in great detail in a blog posting from 2004 (Allen 2004).

Since we are faced with similar challenges in Enterprise 2.0, it is entirely reasonable for us to examine the findings of previous activities concerned with studying the support for cooperative work between members of a particular organization.A number of particularly interesting lessons from the past can be taken from work in the field of CSCW; for example, an improved understanding of the differences – and the similarities – between the use of traditional groupware and social software within a business.

Where it all began …

The origins of computer-supported collaborative work (CSCW) as a research discipline can be traced back to the early 1980s. The term 'CSCW' itself was first used as the title of a workshop organized by Irene Greif and Paul Cashman.

Held in Endicot House, Massachusetts in 1984, this workshop brought together people working in a variety of research disciplines, with the aim of exchanging ideas and research results on the use of computers to support collaborative work.

Since then, a number of technologies and tools have been developed and tested within the CSCW field of study. At the same time, however, fundamental contributions to our understanding of communication and cooperation were also being made, including work on the process of introducing tools to support both these activities. One set of findings from the work in CSCW involves the characterization of social interactions within groups, for example. In this context, the relevant work in this area generally differentiates between the following five forms of social interaction between individuals within groups: coexistence, communication, coordination, consensus, and collaboration (see e.g., Koch/Gross 2006).

Coexistence is itself the central precondition for teamwork; we will revisit this concept later on in our discussion. Communication lets us form agreements, exchange ideas, and circulate information. Coordination is necessary if dependencies exist between the activities of different group participants (Malone/Crowston 1992). Consensus is understood to mean the group decision-making process. Finally, collaboration describes the actual act of teamwork itself: the collective manipulation of distributed resources. While communication can be either direct (message recipients are known at the time of sending) or indirect (message recipients have not been finalized at the time of sending), effective cooperation is itself only possible if many people can coordinate their access to common artifacts and are also aware of their coexistence.

The CSCW community has, for example, developed a model – the "People/Artifact Framework" – to help define the various possible forms of communication within a group. This model is centered on the functional relationships between group members as well as the tools for supporting collaboration, depicting these relationships in a way that allows system designers to trace the flow of information within the system (Dix et al. 1993, p. 465). Figure 1 shows the core of the framework. The directional and bidirectional arrows indicate channels of communication that exist between people or between people and work artifacts.

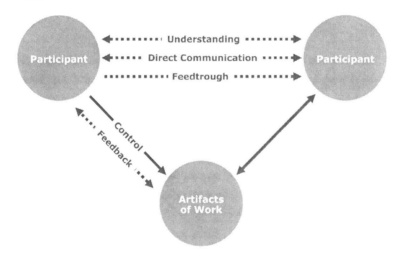

Figure 1: People/Artifact framework

Computer systems designed to support collaboration are often referred to as 'groupware.' In their article "Groupware: Software for Computer-Supported Cooperative Work," Marca and Bock (1992, p. 60) point out that the development of groupware does not itself constitute a further evolutionary stage in the history of IT, but is instead

„a conceptual shift; a shift in our understanding. The traditional computing paradigm sees the computer as a tool for manipulating and exchanging data. The groupware paradigm, on the other hand, views the computer as a shared space in which people collaborate; a clear shift in the relationship between people and information."

Thus, groupware is not characterized by any of its several applications that may themselves incorporate collaborative aspects. The computer should not be seen as a medium for the processing of information, but, instead, as a medium for communication and cooperation. These key attributes for computers were themselves foreseen many decades ago by visionaries such as Vannevar Bush, Douglas Engelbart, and Joseph Carl Robnett Licklider. Initial signs of this new direction in thought appeared in 1945, in Bush's seminal article "As We May Think." In his essay, Bush describes a system called „Memex," which enables the storage of large volumes of data. He recommends constructing an organizational system with associative storage and paths through the data, to ensure that navigation through the volumes of data remains possible (Bush 1945).

While one of Bush's predictions – that microfilm would become the dominant medium for data storage – has obviously not come to pass, he was nonetheless entirely accurate in anticipating systems that would be able to provide greater quantities of data than could be efficiently organized by humankind. With his concept of substantial, shared, and structured information storage systems (typified by the present-day World Wide Web), Bush inspired many later researchers, among them Douglas Engelbart from the Stanford Research Institute, whose team has worked with Bush's ideas, using new techniques to develop them further.

Within the scope of their work on augmenting the human intellect, Engelbart and English (1968) made the recommendation that computers and humans should develop in parallel. Both authors viewed computers and their software as tools for augmenting the range of human potential, not for replacing it. In their theory, Engelbart and his team define four basic kinds of augmentation: artifacts – physical objects designed to provide for human comfort, for the manipulation of things or materials, and the manipulation of symbols; language; methodology; and training (Bornschein-Grass 1995, p. 51).

At the Fall Joint Computer Conference of the International Federation of Information Processing (IFIP) held in San Francisco in 1968, Engelbart demonstrated his prototype of a collaborative application. As a result of its far-reaching impact and the many innovative ideas that were showcased within it, this demonstration has often been referred to as "The Mother of All Demos." Although Engelbart and his team had to build their system from scratch (none of the standard modern development tools, application frameworks, or toolkits were available at the time) this early system nonetheless evidences many of what are today regarded as key principles, including the separation of the application from the user interface plus the use of hypertext models and remote procedure calls (Engelbart/English 1968). Engelbart focused the majority of his research on the subject of human collaboration. Contemporary theory would classify portions of his work as studies on the human factor in computing and thus assign them to the area of human-computer interaction (HCI). His research also led him to equip his prototypes with new features such as windows, icons, combined text and graphics, pop-up menus, and mouse-like input devices (Engelbart 1963; Engelbart/English 1968).

This period also saw the emergence of theories on collaboration and knowledge transfer within virtual communities. As early as 1968, Joseph Carl Robnett Licklider – himself a major influence on the development on the Internet – wrote the following: „Life will be happier for the on-line individual because the people with whom one interacts most strongly will be selected more by commonality of interests and goals than by accidents of proximity." (Licklider/Taylor 1968).

Developments in the 1980s indicated that it was becoming increasingly important to produce models capable of understanding the increased availability of networked computers both at home and at work as well as the possibilities that they were offering for computer-supported communication and coordination. Grudin (1991, p. 93) is not alone in citing the following conditions as fostering research and development within CSCW:

- Computers have become affordable for all members of a group.

- A technical infrastructure of networks and network software is available.

- Participants are now expert users of this hardware and software.

Initially, researchers in CSCW focused their studies on small groups. While social, political, and motivational aspects had gone largely unnoticed during the development of systems for individual use, these factors became of central importance when considered in the scope of groupware.

CSCW and the work system

In providing support for collaboration, the primary consideration is not the provisioning of technologies and tools but the design and structure of 'socio-technical' systems. The term socio-technical system was coined in the 1950s by Trist and Bamforth (1951), working at the Tavistock Institute in London. At the time, they were studying the organization of work in the British coal and textile industries (see also Emery/Trist 1960). Analyzing their studies, the researchers saw that different working groups produced different results, even though the technologies introduced were identical. The key insight arising from their analyses of the data was that the technical and social aspects of a system must be optimized in concert to ensure the smooth functioning of the whole. Where a technical solution is introduced without taking the social system into account, the results will be suboptimal. Although the original work on socio-technical systems constituted traditional workplace studies, the models it produced were later adopted and adapted to the use of computer-based information systems and their support for social groups (Mumford 1987). Here, the technical system comprises (networked) computers and software, while the social system is made up of the group of users, the organization in which they work, and the relationships between group members.

In occupational psychology, the term "work system" is used for a socio-technical system that represents clearly identifiable, discrete sub-systems within an organization or a business enterprise. According to the models from occupational psychology, work systems are made up of the following components (Sydow 1985):

- Persons with qualifications, interests, and needs

- Technology (machinery, computer systems, work resources)

- Organization and structure (workflows, systems for decision-making and communication)

- A primary goal for the work system

The primary goal of the work system is of paramount importance for the whole system, since it is both a source of motivation and a force that binds the system together. Research in CSCW has made extensive use of these insights into the design of systems for supporting collaborative work. For CSCW, the key insights arising from the discourse on socio-technical systems are:

- Technical systems are inseparably interconnected with social systems.

- Social and technical sub-systems should be designed (optimized) in concert, since they influence one another.

- Priority must be given to the goal of the system as a whole: it will normally constitute the central source of cohesion for the system.

The existence of interdependencies makes socio-technical systems highly complex – something that should be taken into account in the design process. For example, it is unlikely that the perfect solution will be found at the first attempt.

This point of view highlights the interdependency of social and technical systems very well. While social processes are the basis for the development of technologies, technologies in turn structure the possibilities for social interaction (Mumford 2000). Accordingly, research in CSCW is concerned with understanding the patterns of social interaction between teams, communities, and networks while also prototyping, developing, and evaluating technical systems that can themselves support social interaction. Many definitions are available for the term 'CSCW.' A highly generalized definition is adopted by Bowers and Benford (1991, p. 5): „In its most general form, CSCW examines the possibilities and effects of technological support for humans involved in collaborative group communication and work processes.“

Other researchers place greater emphasis on group work / group activity within CSCW. Wilson (1991), for example, defines the term as follows: „CSCW is a generic term which combines the understanding of the way people work in groups with the enabling technologies of computer networking, and associated hardware, software, services, and techniques.“

Groupware

While technology and tools are not the only element to be considered when designing socio-technical systems for supporting collaborative work, they nonetheless have an important role to play. This technology and its tools are generally referred to as "groupware." In contrast to traditional computer systems that are primarily developed for a single, individual user, the main aim of groupware is to support the activities of a group of users in the areas of communication, collaboration, and coordination. Ellis, Jacobson, and Horvitz (1991, p. 40) describe groupware in the following way: "Groupware are computer-based systems that support groups of people engaged in a common task (or goal) and that provide an interface to a shared environment."

Figure 2 gives an overview of the classification of groupware in accordance with primary interaction types that it supports. However, when it comes to preferences for systems of categorization, researchers are divided, with less common agreement on where distributed systems end and groupware begins – i.e., how groupware itself differs from other (distributed) systems.

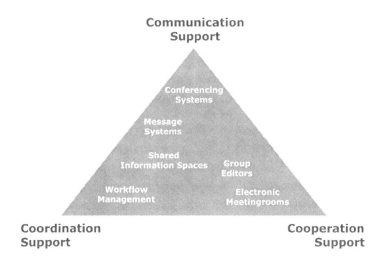

Figure 2: Classification of groupware according to the primary interaction types supported – communication, coordination and cooperation (3c model)

One approach to the categorization of groupware is to assume that the chief characteristic of groupware lies in its explicit attempt to reduce the extent to which users are isolated from one another. This would mean that groupware is characterized by its role in making users more aware of their colleagues and their activities. This theory has been propounded by Lynch et al. (1990, p. 160):

Groupware is distinguished from normal software by the basic assumption it makes: Groupware makes the user aware that he is part of a group, while most other software seeks to hide and protect users from each other [...]

Groupware [...] is software that accentuates the multiple user environment, coordinating and orchestrating things so that users can 'see' each other, yet do not conflict with each other."

A second key characteristic that has been identified for groupware is the ease with which it can be customized. Since every group is different, and groupware must not only serve the needs of the group as a whole but also the requirements of each and every individual within this group in order to activate a critical mass of users, there is generally a low likelihood that one solution will solve every potential problem. Groupware must be highly generic. It must provide a medium that users and their groups can utilize for a number of different purposes (e-mail is the best example of this medium-focused aspect of groupware). Ideally, the users themselves will be able to perform any necessary customization. Research in this field goes by the name of "end-user development" (Lieberman et al. 2006).

In addition to the viewpoint held by CSCW research, there is also another "definition" of the term groupware: in the specialist computer media and the software industry, groupware is often used as a synonym for Microsoft Outlook/Exchange or similar packages based on the MAPI protocol. This definition restricts groupware to providing the following functionality: e-mail, (group) calendar, (group) address book, and (group) task list management. While this may well cover the functional scope of early commercial groupware, this definition is no longer up-to-date.

A number of authors have analyzed CSCW projects and identified requirements critical in the design of collaborative systems as opposed to the development of general software systems. The reader is referred here to the early work of Ellis et al. (1991) or Grudin (1988, 1989). Grudin, for example, identifies the following challenges inherent in designing collaborative systems:

- A number of factors hinder the specification of requirements for CSCW systems: first, the wealth of different properties evidenced by groups and standpoints must be analyzed – which is atypical work for a software architect; second, requirements are often not clear even to the future users of the system; third and finally, working parameters are liable to change either during development or as the system is being introduced.

- For a CSCW system to be successful, the system must be actively used either by all of the group members or at least a significant proportion of them (network effect, critical mass). The ratio of effort required to use the system to the benefit derived from using it must always be reasonable. This must be established via a positive cost-benefit analysis for all users – which must then also be communicated to all users of the system.

A number of approaches addressing these inherent challenges have been proposed concerning the introduction of CSCW systems. These solutions focus especially on the areas of requirements analysis and change management – i.e., the implementation and/or introduction of CSCW systems.

Participatory and evolutionary development within CSCW

At the outset, an iterative or 'evolutionary' development process was established, in order to help grasp the elusive and rapidly-changing requirements of such systems. Such evolutionary models of system development are based on the principle of executing the tasks of requirements analysis, design, and implementation not simply on one, but on multiple occasions. In addition to this evolutionary design process, the participation of users and other interested stakeholders in all phases of development must also be assured: initially passive spectators of the system, prospective users then become directly involved in its development. Involving the system's users in this way not only aids in correctly assessing requirements but also helps ensure a favorable environment for the new system – a tactic utilized in successful change management strategies.

In connection with this, it is important to note that 'implementing a system' in CSCW always refers to the design of a complete, socio-technical system – covering both the design of the organizational and social aspects of the system as well as the integration of the technical system into the various work processes. Indeed, CSCW now focuses primarily on issues of integration into social systems, since the technical system itself generally no longer needs to be implemented completely from scratch, but can instead be constructed and configured using standard components.

Research on CSCW provides us with a toolbox backed up by experience that is of great use in designing and implementing these kinds of information systems, which provide functions supporting collaborative work within an organization. In order to systematically identify social and organizational requirements while also achieving an understanding of the methodology itself, a number of ethnographical methodologies have been used, modified to suit the workplace scenario (e.g., see Blomberg et al. 1993; Jordan 1996). The focus here was on observing the users acting within their normal work environment. Ethnography is thus able to discover work patterns that would not otherwise come to light if users were to be directly asked about their ways of working.

"As practiced by most ethnographers, developing an understanding of human behavior requires a period of field work where the ethnographer becomes immersed in the activities of the people studied. Typically, field work involves some combination of observation, informal interviewing, and participation in the ongoing events of the community. Through extensive contact with the people studied, ethnographers develop a descriptive understanding of the observed behaviors" (Blomberg et al. 1993, p. 124).

A variety of participatory design methods have been developed to encourage the active involvement of users (Schuler/Namioka 1993; Muller/Kuhn 1993). "The focus of participatory design (PD) is not only the improvement of the information system, but also the empowerment of workers so they can co-determine the development of the information system and of their workplace" (Clement/Van den Besselaar 1993, p. 93).

Participatory design is thus a method complementary to ethnography, since it involves users and other interested stakeholders being actively involved in the entire lifecycle of system development from its earliest stages onwards. One example of a participatory design method is the socio-technical 'walkthrough' (Herrmann et al. 2004, 2007). This method involves organizing a number of moderated workshops in which the complete socio-technical system is initially discussed – and subsequently developed – by its own users. Definitions of socio-technical systems are themselves drawn up using a specialized modeling methodology that extends standard system modeling languages such as UML by providing specific constructs for use in mapping socio-technological systems (Loser/Herrmann 2001).

The advent of Web 2.0, Social Software and Enterprise 2.0

This section does not provide a detailed description of the historical and conceptual aspects – these can be found in other chapters of this book. Instead, I summarize here what I consider to be the most important characteristics of this development. The most often-quoted definition of Web 2.0 is that given by Tim O'Reilly in his article "What is Web 2.0" (2005). In his essay, O'Reilly characterizes Web 2.0 (in comparison to Web 1.0) as

- An architecture of participation

- Data sources that can be freely combined

- Services that are simple to configure and integrate – in contrast with monolithic software packages

The most important concept in relation to this definition is the level of participation that is attained by the free cooperation of as many users as possible, unhindered by organizational or structural aspects, or by limitations of technologies or systems. Two further principles are often named as essential in achieving this level of participation:

- Sufficient usability for services is achieved through the implementation of Web-based services and interactivity.

- The "me"-centered services focus on the utility of the service for the individual user. Intrinsic motivation thus has a large part to play here. Real service value can be understood only in the context of a team or a community.

Social software is often characterized as a subset of Web 2.0: software or services that support, enhance, or generate additional value from human social interaction (Coates 2005). Here we observe a conceptual similarity with Web 2.0: while the computer is used as a medium for communication and cooperation, the primary focus is on the individual user and not on the group – as is the case with groupware.

As stated earlier, discussions involving the utilization of computers as a social medium were underway well before the advent of Web 2.0 – as evident from the work of Bush, Engelbart, and Licklider, for example.

Indeed, even the term itself is not entirely new. A program of research entitled "The Social Web" had already been proposed by Peter Hoschka in 1998, long before the appearance of the term 'social software' (Hoschka 1998). Clay Shirky, the 'inventor' of the term social software, admits that he chose the term with the following in mind: "[I was] looking for something that gathered together all uses of software that supported interacting groups, even if the interaction was offline."

Justifying his decision not to use the term 'collaborative software,' Shirky explains: "Because that seems a sub-set of Groupware, leaving out other kinds of group processes such as [...] play." Andrew McAfee (2006) sums up the typical characteristics of social software in his acronym SLATES: search, links, authoring, tags, extensibility, signals. Koch and Richter (2008, p. 14) make use of a slightly-modified version of this definition:

- Enable simple self-publication of articles or content editing ("authoring")

- Support contributions via tagging or structured metadata ("tags")

- Enable simple publication of additional content and metadata via annotation and/or linking ("authoring," "links")

- Ensure awareness of content updates via subscriptions for newly-published content ("signals")

- Implement simple content discovery ("search," "tags")

- Build applications as modular, service-oriented structures ("extensions")

In addition to these core qualities, there are also a number of fundamental application types that can be identified within social software – such as wikis or blogs. Using the format of the 3C model for groupware (Figure 2), here we position the application types for social software within a triangle that presents a number of use cases at each apex: information management, identity and network management, and communication (see Figure 3).

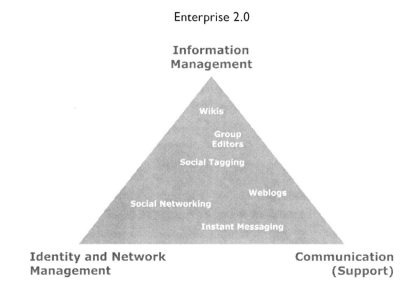

Figure 3: The social software triangle

The social software triangle gives us an overview of the potential uses of social software for supporting collaborative work – whether within the company or between the business and its partners and customers. Andrew McAfee (2006) names this model 'Enterprise 2.0.'

Enterprise 2.0 and CSCW

When comparing social software with groupware, a number of dissimilarities become apparent:

- Orientation on the group (in groupware) vs. communication oriented on the individual (in social software) differentiates between an "us"-centered and a "me"-centered focus.

- Top-down implementation and mandatory participation (in groupware) stands in contrast to bottom-up implementation and optional participation (in social software).

- Groupware assumes control via administrators; social software is based on conventions reached by mutual consensus.

- While on the one hand we have a small group of users and a predefined timeframe (groupware), on the other we have a large number of users who are not bound by any project restrictions (social software).

One should however bear in mind that a more detailed analysis points to a new generation of groupware, which is no longer limited to individual projects and a small number of participants. It is also true that CSCW has always insisted on the importance of freedom of action for users and the need to focus on intrinsic motivation, while recommending that solutions are worked on with (or by) the users. On the other hand, social software itself needs to be considered in the light of the limitations present within the business environment. Accordingly, the only remaining difference between the two is that social software and Enterprise 2.0 concentrate on the individual and a bottom-up implementation, while groupware and early knowledge management projects place their focus on teams and communities.

Once we have concluded that there is more common ground than not between the two systems, we should draw on experience gained working on groupware and CSCW in order to address the challenges that result from the primary differences between Enterprise 2.0 and social software in an Internet context, namely: how to anchor social software tools within a business environment and its inherent organizational structures. This is an important point to consider since structures will continue to persist within companies and there will always be platforms that need to be accommodated in the process of introducing social software tools. A couple of recommendations are useful in squaring up to these challenges:

1. Stay as close as possible to the optimal "me"-centered focal point and bottom-up introduction of social software.

2. If this is not possible, then one should heed the advice of CSCW and introduce the tools in a manner that is as participative and lightweight as possible.

One observation concerning the first recommendation and a question that often arises in discussions on Enterprise 2.0: is it necessary for a company to change itself in order to extract the full range of benefits from implementing the Enterprise 2.0 toolset? Such discussions consider Enterprise 2.0 not only as a collection of cutting-edge tools but also as a "new kind of company." Corporate culture should certainly develop in a way that results in the retention of as few impediments as possible in the form of structures and hierarchies. Staff should be granted as much freedom of action as possible.

Some structures will necessarily need to be retained however – otherwise the organization will of course cease to be a company in the conventional sense. In order to achieve the greatest team and company benefit, employees will need to coordinate their activities and work towards establishing a system of mutual collaboration. Here it is possible to approach the optimum use of social software by ensuring that employees are involved as closely as possible in the design of the workplace and in the definition of necessary structures. This calls for a participatory design process for the entire socio-technical system complete with its supportive technologies, while also acknowledging the organizational and social aspects of the total system.

This brings us to our second recommendation: prioritize participation and evolutionary/iterative processes when modifying or introducing systems. If one wants to provide a team with a wiki, then all team members should be involved in the project from its inception onwards. Ideally, one would start the ball rolling with a discussion during a normal team meeting, ensuring that staff have identified the problem that the project intends to solve. This discussion must also include an identification of processes and other systems affected. It sometimes happens that a simple, non-technical solution is identified during this phase – or, alternatively, the discovery is made that the actual problem is something quite different entirely. Should it be the case that a technical solution is still under consideration, then one should achieve consensus within the team on the following points of order: 1. Where will the tool be used, and which processes will need to be changed to accommodate it? 2. What contribution to the implementation will be required of each team member – not just during implementation, but during actual productive use? 3. What is the expected benefit for each participant in the solution? Finally, the solution should be the subject of regular assessments during team meetings, and, where necessary, should either be modified or retired as appropriate.

The importance of utilizing bottom-up techniques for the introduction of groupware can also be appreciated if one looks at the status of groupware within the IT architecture typically found within business. Groupware normally occupies a position between personal productivity software – where the value for the individual and the motivation of the individual is of extreme importance – and large-scale solutions (e.g., ERP systems), where the support of management is a critical factor for the success of the system. Groupware resembles the large-scale system in that it is a solution that needs to be adjusted to personal requirements, while it must also be capable of stimulating a variety of group responses. On the other hand, the low cost of groupware means that it tends to have only low visibility within large organizations. Grudin and Palen (1995) used group calendaring systems to study both of these aspects, identifying a number of cases where clear bottom-up patterns were evident during system deployment.

This discussion also reveals a further challenge facing those attempting to realize CSCW or Enterprise 2.0 concepts: motivation. This is one of the most important teachings from CSCW: strive to achieve a balance between effort and benefit in order to guarantee a high user acceptance rate. While the ideal scenario may forecast a positive benefit for every user, this is unfortunately not always attainable under real-world conditions. A high level of motivation, however, offers the possibility of compensating for any extra effort required. Fundamental research in the field of social systems has yielded insights describing the differences between intrinsic and extrinsic motivation (Frey/Osterloh 2002). Extrinsic motivation is derived from external rewards, while intrinsic motivation comes from internal factors such as job satisfaction and identification with shared values. In the context of social software platforms, it has proven counterproductive to pay users directly for their collaboration or to link specific activities directly to payments ('crowding-out effect'). The explanation given is that these actions irretrievably replace the natural intrinsic motivation to participate (Frey/Osterloh 2002). Accordingly, any steps taken to increase motivation should always focus on strengthening intrinsic motivation. This can be done by granting workers more freedom of action, for example, or by ensuring that staff achieve greater prominence as a result of greater appreciation.

Conclusions

The Web presents us with the ideal infrastructure for supporting collaborative work. Not only has it made its presence felt throughout society, it has also made available a number of ubiquitous and homogenous protocols (HTTP), formats (HTML, etc.) and software (Web browsers), which together provide the majority of potential system users with easy access to services supporting collaboration. With ever-increasing available bandwidth and the relentless march of technological development, the Web is now eminently suited for use as a medium for cooperation both outside and inside the corporate organization.

In this essay, I have placed Enterprise 2.0 – the use of Web-based social software tools within the enterprise – in its wider context, and also introduced a field of study that has much common ground with Enterprise 2.0, namely Computer-Supported Collaborative Work (CSCW). Since Enterprise 2.0 – unlike 'pure' social software – also displays a number of top-down aspects, the many years of experience in the field of CSCW may well be able to contribute to ensuring its success.

This experience can generally be said to have achieved an understanding of the ways groups and organizations function, and how technical systems can best be introduced in order to support these ways of working. Not only can CSCW for Enterprise 2.0 provide the theoretical basis for collaboration and the various forms it assumes, but it can also supply practical know-how concerning the design of cooperative systems. CSCW experience also warns us that the provisioning of support for collaboration can never be carried out using a top-down model alone. A policy of user involvement, a system development model that takes into account the benefit for each and every user and the granting of freedom of action for users constitute the central factors for success in supporting collaborative work.

WORKS CITED

Allen, C. (2004): Tracing the Evolution of Social Software. Life with Alacrity Blog. http://www.lifewithalacrity.com/2004/10/tracing_the_evo.html

Blomberg, J.; Giacomi, J.; Mosher, A.; Swenton-Wall, P. (1993): Ethnographic field methods and their relation to design. In: Schuler, D.; Namioka, A. (eds.), Participatory Design: Perspectives on System Design, Hillsdale, NJ: Lawrence Erlbaum Associates, pp. 123-154.

Bornschein-Grass, C. (1995): Groupware und computergestützte Zusammenarbeit: Wirkungsbereiche und Potentiale, Wiesbaden: Gabler.

Bowers, J. ; Benford, S. D. (eds.) (1991): Studies in Computer-Supported Co-operative Work: Theory, Practice, and Design - Human Factors in Information Technology, Amsterdam: Elsevier Science.

Bush, V. (1945): As We May Think. In: The Atlantic Monthly, 176 (1), pp. 101-108.

Clement, A.; Van den Besselaar, P. (1993): A retrospective look at PD projects. In: Communications of the ACM, 36 (6), pp. 29-37.

Coates, T. (2005): An addendum to a definition of Social Software. http://www.plasticbag.org/archives/2005/01/an_ addendum_to_ a_ definition_ of_social_software. Last accessed May 11, 2007.

Dix, A. J.; Finley, J.; Abowd, G. D.; Beale, R. (1993): Human-Computer Interaction. New York: Prentice Hall.

Ellis, C. A.; Gibbs, S. J.; Rein, G. L. (1991): Groupware – Some Issues and Experiences. Communications of the ACM, 34 (1), pp. 38-58.

Emery, F. E.; Trist, E. L. (1960): Socio-Technical Systems. In: Churchman, C. W. (ed.): Management Sciences, Models and Techniques, London: Pergamon.

Engelbart, D. C. (1963): A Conceptual Framework for the Augmentation of Man's Intellect. In: Information Handling, Volume 1, Washington, DC: Spartan Books.

Engelbart, D. C.; English, W. K. (1968): A Research Center for Augmenting Human Intellect. In: Proceedings of the Fall Joint Computing Conference – FJCC'68 (Montvale, NY), AFIPS Press, pp. 395-410.

Frey, B. S.; Osterloh, M. (2002): Motivation - A Dual-Edged Factor of Production. In: Frey, B. S.; Osterloh, M. (eds.): Successful Management by Motivation. Berlin: Springer, pp. 3-26.

Gross, T.; Koch, M. (2007): Computer-Supported Cooperative Work. Munich: Oldenbourg Wissenschaftsverlag.

Grudin, J. (1988): Why CSCW applications fail: Problems in the design and evaluation of organizational interfaces. In: Proc. Conf. on Computer-Supported Cooperative Work (CSCW), ACM Press, pp. 85-93.

Grudin, J. (1989): Why Groupware applications fail: Problems in design and evaluation. Office: Technology and People, 4 (3), pp. 245-264.

Grudin, J. (1991): CSCW: The Convergence of Two Development Contexts. In: Proc. Conf. on Human Factors in Computing Systems (CHI), ACM Press, pp. 261-268.

Grudin, J.; Palen, L. (1995): Why Groupware Succeeds: Discretion or Mandate? In: Proc. Europ. Conf. on Computer-Supported Cooperative Work (Stockholm, Sweden), Kluwer, pp. 85-93.

Herrmann, T.; Kunau, G.; Loser, K.-U.; Menold, N. (2004): Socio-Technical Walk- through: Designing Technology along Work Processes. In: Proc. Participatory Design Conference (PDC), pp. 132-141.

Herrmann, T.; Loser, K.-U.; Jahnke, I. (2007): Socio-technical Walk-through (STWT): a Means for Knowledge Integration. In: International Journal of Learning Organization. Special Issue: Solving Problems in Knowledge Sharing with Sociotechnical Approaches. E. Coakes; Ramirez, A. (eds.).

Hoschka, P. (1998): Der Computer als soziales Medium. In: GMD-Spiegel 3/4 (28), S. 16-19.

Jordan, B. (1996): Ethnographic workplace studies and CSCW. In: Shapiro, D.; Tauber, M.; Traunmüller, R. (eds.), The Design of Computer Supported Cooperative Work and Groupware Systems, Amsterdam: Elsevier Science, pp. 17-42.

Koch, M.; Gross, T. (2006): Computer-Supported Cooperative Work – Concepts and Trends. In: Proc. Conf. of the Association Information and Management (AIM), Lecture Notes in Informatics (LNI) P-92, Bonn: Koellen Verlag.

Koch, M.; Richter, A. (2008): Enterprise 2.0 - Planung, Einführung und erfolgreicher Einsatz von Social Software im Unternehmen. Munich: Oldenbourg Wissenschaftsverlag.

Licklider, J. C. R.; Taylor, R. (1968): The Computer as a Communication Device. Science and Technology 76, pp. 21-31.

Lieberman, H.; Paterno, F.; Wulf, V. (eds.) (2006): End-User Development. Dordrecht, The Netherlands: Springer, Human-Computer Interaction Series Vol. 9.

Loser, K.-U.; Herrmann, T. (2001): Diagrammatic Models for Participatory Design of Socio-Technical Systems. In: Bjornestad, S.; Moe, R.; Morch, A.; Opdahl, A.: IRIS 24. Proceedings of the 24th Information Systems Research Seminar in Scandinavia, pp. 285-300.

Lynch, K. J.; Snyder, J. M.; Vogel, D. M.; McHenry, W. K. (1990): The Arizona Analyst Information System: Supporting Collaborative Research on International Technological Trends. In: Gibbs, S.; Verrijn-Stuart, A. A.: Multi-User Interfaces and Applications, Amsterdam: Elsevier Science, pp. 159-174

Malone, T. W.; Crowston, K. (1992): Towards an Interdisciplinary Theory of Co- ordination. Technical Report CSS TR#120, Cambridge: Center for Coordination Science, Sloan School of Management, Massachusetts Institute of Technology.

Marca, D.; Bock, G. (eds.) (1992): Groupware: Software for Computer-Supported Cooperative Work. Los Almitos: IEE Press.

McAfee, A. (2006): Enterprise 2.0: The Dawn of Emergent Collaboration. MIT Sloan Management Review 47 (3): pp. 21-28.

Muller, M. J.; Kuhn, S. (eds.) (1993): Special Issue on Participatory Design. In: Communications of the ACM, 36 (6), pp. 24-28.

Mumford, E. (1987): Socio-technical Systems Design – Evolving theory and practice. In: Bjerknes, G.; Ehn, P.; Kyng, S. (eds.): Computers and Democracy: A Scandinavian Challenge, Aldershot: Avebury, pp. 59-77.

Mumford, E. (2000): A Socio-technical Approach to Systems Design. In: Requirements Engineering 5, pp. 125-133.

O'Reilly, T. (2005): What Is Web 2.0 - Design Patterns and Business Models for the Next Generation of Software. http://www.oreillynet.com/pub/a/oreilly/tim/news/2005/09/30/what-is-web-20.html. Last accessed Jan 5, 2007.

Schuler, D.; Namioka, A. (1993): Participatory Design: Principles and Practices. Hillsdale, NJ: Lawrence Erlbaum.

Sydow, J. (1985): Organisationsspielraum und Büroautomation. Berlin: De Gruyter.

Trist, E.; Bamforth, K. (1951): Some social and psychological consequences of the long wall method of coal getting. In: Human Relations 4, pp. 3-38.

Wilson, P. (1991): Computer Supported Cooperative Work: An Introduction, Oxford, UK: Intellect Books.

Sören Stamer
Enterprise 2.0 - Learning by Doing

Your advantage

It is surely uncontroversial to state that the Internet is a dramatic force for change in our world. However, the ultimate magnitude and significance of these changes remains a subject of interested speculation and discussion. As an entrepreneur in the fast-moving software industry, I became convinced that the disruptive effects of these changes would transform companies in a far more fundamental way than contemporary opinion would have us believe.

And the disruptive effects of the Internet are spreading at breathtaking speed, questioning tried-and-tested business models, ways of working, organizational structures, and even accepted truths – and not just in the software industry. The best forecasts predict that this trend will continue apace – or even "worsen" – since the processes involved are exponential. Not only does processor speed double every eighteen months, in accordance with Moore's Law (amounting to a thousandfold increase every fifteen years): our total knowledge is also growing exponentially. New ideas and processes bringing change are spreading at an exponential rate.

And exponential curves are dangerous things, fundamentally changing the rules of play. As such, they present company management with an existential challenge: How can one stay in control of a company when the market, the technologies in use, global competition, and society itself is changing at an ever-increasing rate? In the following pages, I look forward to sharing with you my experiences so far in answering this question for my own company and the events that took place on the road that we set out on – the road to *Enterprise 2.0*. Perhaps it may well lead to a productive dialogue with many positive network effects. That would give me great satisfaction.

As a manager, if you can answer the following four questions with a decisive "Yes," then you have my unqualified admiration:

Can you say without a shadow of a doubt that your company is innovative enough to achieve long-term success in the future?

Would you say that your company is currently utilizing and developing the potential of all of your staff members in an optimal way?

Is your company such a great place to work that all of your teams are mastering new challenges in a highly-motivated, highly creative way – and on a daily basis?

Can you unequivocally identify yourself with your company and its purpose?

Hopefully your answers have given you food for thought. I'll hazard a guess that for at least three of the four questions, you will have had your doubts. If you did, then you are not alone (leaving startups out of the picture). I felt the exact same way only a short while ago. At the beginning of 2005, I also realized – very suddenly, in fact – that for CoreMedia AG, the company at which I have been CEO since 1996, my honest answer for three of the four questions would also have been "No" – even despite the fact that turnover and profit were both coming along just fine. It was a shock. A particularly painful kind of shock. And yet a beneficial one, too, since it provided the groundwork for a fundamental change for the better. Looking back, it was the catalyst for CoreMedia's evolution into an *Enterprise 2.0*.

An *Enterprise 2.0* differs from an Enterprise 1.0 by virtue of its attitude towards and its usage of the kinds of successful self-organization that enable a company to exist. While an Enterprise 1.0 is characterized by the use of hierarchical structures and processes to increase performance, Enterprise 2.0 involves adopting the reverse strategy: hierarchies are deliberately broken down in many places in order to create the necessary space for the operation of successful self-organization. The successful introduction of self-organization releases an enduring innovative power and creativity that enables output to be boosted many times over, rather than just increasing it a few percent at a time. So, if there is such a thing as a motto for the change to Enterprise 2.0, then it must be "the art of letting go."

The greatest obstacle on the path to improving companies and their chances of survival is our widely-adopted and deeply-held belief in hierarchical structures, fine-tuned processes, and far-sighted decision-makers, as well as our inability to imagine that success can also be achieved via alternative organizational models that are held to be counter-intuitive (Reihlen 1998, p.3). In 2005, CoreMedia set out on its quest to reduce this blind spot, systematically searching for new and improved solutions far removed from traditional hierarchies. This journey wasn't always an easy one for us. In the following pages, you can read about the experience I gained first-hand as CEO of CoreMedia AG.. I focus on the specific patterns for success that have already proven to be both dependable and transferable. I do, however, highlight our errors along the way – which indeed are on occasion far more illuminating than our successes.

The blind spot: self-organization does work

For me personally, the change process described had begun some nine months earlier, at the beginning of 2004. Attending a three-day seminar in Salzburg with seven other entrepreneurs and management staff, I saw how a group that started out as complete strangers could form a team and then proceed to work in an entirely self-organized fashion. At the end, our mutual accomplishments stunned and fascinated the participants in equal measure: the productivity and creativity shown by our newly-formed team was far greater than what we would normally experience – as was the fun we had while working.

The secret obviously lay in the design of the workshop. Preconditions were kept to a minimum, specifying only the goal of the workshop, some general rules about how the goal was to be reached (in three stages), the time available, plus the fact that all participants were to be considered as equals. The rest developed out of self-organization. The seminar coach took very great pains to avoid assuming the role of "leader" – or to have such a role thrust upon him. He remained at a distance, monitoring events as an observer. Only when the group agreed unanimously that they were unable to resolve a particular issue did the trainer come in as a consultant to offer the group a way of solving the problem. Thus, the obvious tendency of the participants to transfer responsibility to the seminar coach in times of indecision – and to develop a dependency on his judgment – was circumvented in a highly effective manner. The group was forced to handle conflict themselves and matured as part of this self-learning process.

This seminar demonstrated to me the powerful forces for creativity and design that can be set free within self-organized systems. I was fascinated by the levels of vitality and output that a self-organized team can command – and remain so to this day. I immediately began to investigate these forces, the conditions that made them possible, and the fundamental processes for self-organization. As I conducted my research, I thought constantly about how I could set free these extraordinary forces in my own company.

It wasn't long before I realized that I was the key to the process. If I wanted to develop my company further, then I first needed to secure my own development. I had to get to work on my personality. Via feedback, reflection, and coaching it became clear to me that my leadership style set the standard against which all others would be measured, namely the way I dealt with power, with rules, with feedback, and with other behavioral forms. I thus provided both cause and solution for the problem.

Self-organization needs space to work in. Then again, self-organization also requires a certain amount of structure in order to achieve success. Yet in the majority of cases, too much structure kills off self-organization before it can even begin to be productive. We know of a number of contemporary examples that show us the connection between space and structure in ways that still surprise and fascinate us. Wikipedia manages without an editor-in-chief, without approval processes, and without access controls for its editors. With a few exceptions, any author can edit any page as he or she sees fit. And despite this – or maybe precisely because of it – Wikipedia quickly grew into the largest encyclopedia in the world, available in over 150 languages and boasting impressive levels of quality. The German Brockhaus publishing house has recently reacted to this development with the announcement that it is not planning to produce further print editions of the famous Brockhaus encyclopedia[8]. I assume that Wikipedia will continue to improve on its service and will probably locate patterns that lead to even greater improvements in quality, without hindering the dynamism that drives the project. Other examples of remarkable results from self-organized systems are presented by our culture and our language, global trade, open source projects, and even the life on this planet itself.

"Best Innovator" and yet still too slow

In 2004, CoreMedia was recognized as "Best Innovator" among German SME companies. Together with BMW, the winner in the major enterprise category, we accepted the prize from AT Kearney and the magazine *Wirtschaftswoche* in recognition of our achievements in innovation management. This distinction was a great honor for CoreMedia, and one that was thoroughly grounded in factual evidence. CoreMedia had brought numerous innovations on to the market over the years, while achieving constant growth – on occasions as much as 150 percent annually – even in the face of the collapse of the "dot-com bubble" in 2000. But was it enough?

Following on from my highly positive experiences with self-organized teams, I had declared it my goal to introduce this way of working at CoreMedia in order to boost our output and our ability to learn. After I had begun to reflect on my leadership style in 2004, it was high time that the entire management team also got involved in the process. In January 2005, I consequently invited my five colleagues from the original management team to attend a two-day strategy meeting. In contrast to earlier work summits of this kind, this time I would be taking on a different role. Instead of working within the team as a normal team member, this time I took on the role of an external adviser. Supervising the whole event was the corporate consultant and coach Ingo Lanzdorf, whose seminar for entrepreneurs I had previously attended.

On the evening before the event, we met for a communal evening meal in the Nordheide[9]. Seated comfortably at the round table, the mood was relaxed and convivial, and in the course of the evening, an interesting assessment was made of the last company Christmas party. Everyone present was convinced that something was wrong: in comparison with the previous years, this Christmas party had been a disappointment. Instead of a host of creative ideas, intelligent games, passionate and rousing speeches, and appreciative feedback, it had been a truly dismal celebration. A conspicuous sign of the palpable unease was the fact that our company band had not played – for the first time since their formation.

We quickly came to the unanimous conclusion that we had not been giving the creative efforts of the teams enough credit in the past. We had not sufficiently honored the work and creativity demonstrated by previous Christmas parties – all of which had been self-organized. Everyone took the criticisms to heart. And suddenly, a highly creative discussion broke out based on this insight, casting about for the right impulse that could accept this criticism and once again show our appreciation. The discussion was exceedingly lively – the conversation went back and forth. One idea followed another, expanding and improving on the original. So, it was almost inevitable that we came up with a plan in next to no time at all:

"Let's stage a public concert to be given by our in-house band at our own CeBIT stand. All our staff members should experience first hand how our company presents itself. At the same time, everyone should be given the opportunity to get a better idea of our market. To ensure we achieve all this, we'll invite all company employees to the upcoming CeBIT in Hanover, and give them a job to do: 'Find out what's most important for CoreMedia, and make us love it.'"

The management team immediately set to work putting the plan into action. Almost our entire staff was bussed over to Hanover. Once they had arrived, our colleagues formed teams and began to analyze the competition, run customer surveys, observe trends, and even directly address customers standing right next to the CeBIT stands hosted by the competition. In the evenings, our house band played to an audience consisting of numerous customers, partners, staff members, and friends. Just one month later, the individual teams presented their often surprisingly creative results to the assembled company. The unexpected highlight was a clever little film with a highly original didactical method – rather like that used in "Sesame Street." This film compared our product to those sold by the competition.

But let's return to the strategy meeting. Sadly, it stopped being playful, creative, and open. By the morning, everything had changed. The main topic of the strategy meeting was: "How to achieve organic growth more successfully." To get us started with our discussions, I began with a meta-question: "What kinds of strategic questions should we be asking ourselves?"

And then I experienced as observer and adviser just how far removed from a real team my management team actually was. It soon became clear to me that we were facing some major challenges ahead. Instead of working together creatively and appreciatively as on the previous evening, I watched as distinct individuals floundered, apparently unable to renew their concentrated collaborative efforts. The impressive team maturity and capability for self-organization that had been demonstrated on the previous evening had disappeared into thin air. Towards the evening, the supervisor presented us with his diagnosis: the team was not a team. The awareness of a common goal was lacking, resulting in a situation where each person represented his or her own area, rather than working to optimize the total result.

The effects were clearly visible: as a company with a highly conventional departmental structure and a participatory management team, we felt that we were rather lacking in agility and the capacity for rapid implementation. Conflicts between the various departments were becoming more frequent. And the situation in the management team was literally a reflection of the problems with the departments. The result was that our company of around 120 staff members had far greater inertia than in previous years. An overwhelming reason for these symptoms was obviously our departmental structure, together with our ways of managing to date. We had a problem. While we were experiencing unstoppable acceleration in the world around us with more dynamic markets and shortened product lifecycles, CoreMedia's growth was slowing down to a crawl. We were therefore presented with a strategic challenge: the very structures that had brought us success in the past had now become a problem we couldn't ignore.

Departments are generally the problem, not the solution

Earlier, it had been only too natural to have an internal structure with departments such as Marketing, Sales, Development, Consulting, and Internal Services. However, it had now become very clear to me that the structure was a real part of the problem and needed to be dismantled if we wanted to become more agile, more market-oriented, and more innovative. Our departments encouraged blinkered points of view, giving rise to communication difficulties and power plays: in short, they were typical corporate departments.

In order to revive the agility and creativity we knew from the early days of the company, we developed a blueprint for a new organizational structure – one that was precisely oriented on the core processes of the company. Instead of letting departmental boundaries divide up process responsibility, we created teams who would be responsible for the whole process. Following this logic, we combined Sales and Consulting into a Solution Center, for example. Each Solution Center is responsible for the whole process – from the first customer contact through to the successful delivery of services and the acquisition of follow-on projects. From the Product Management and Development departments, the Product Center was forged. Each Product Center is responsible for the whole process – from the product idea through to marketing and maintenance.

Areas that had anything to do with communication as their core activity were also brought into the restructuring process. Client Services was born out of the need to gather and process market data more rapidly and more effectively via multiple channels – and also to communicate with that same market. Groups and activities belonging to Client Services include marketing, public relations, trade fairs and events, as well as training, support, documentation and design. All in all, we changed over from a functional division along mechanistic lines to an organizational paradigm (Krönung 2007, p.54ff). Should a Center flourish and grow, then it undergoes cell division. Division lines are drawn on a contextual rather than a functional basis – according to the grouping of customers, sales regions, or product areas.

And the expectations stemming from our reintegration of the functions across process boundaries have been rapidly fulfilled. After an initial consolidation period, a new dynamism was quick to appear in the individual teams. Long-term weak spots could be identified and ironed out by using the new organizational structure. In fact, our market orientation has been significantly improved merely by the emphasis placed on total responsibility. Our individual teams now act far more autonomously, more quickly, and more creatively. And yet the real innovation on the road to Enterprise 2.0 was carried out at another level entirely. This was the division of functional management and personnel development achieved by the introduction of the CoreMedia Competence Centers (CCC).

Competence is critical and should be actively managed

One of the greatest weaknesses of an organization based on hierarchy is its inadequate handling of employee competence. One initial point of criticism worth mentioning is the fact that the work in departments, with its almost slavish over-subscription to one point of view, often produces a state of awareness that is highly blinkered. And if the members of a department also have the vast majority of their contacts within their own department, then this blinkered view will narrow even further. Not only interdepartmental communication suffers, but also the ability to form a holistic view of one's surroundings.

Such an environment can also promote a sense of ownership of a particular staff member, insofar as his or her skills and abilities are only ever viewed in connection with a specific department. This assumed congruity between functional competence and formal organizational structure also promotes the principle of "power by knowledge." Such an environment renders it impossible to utilize the potential of employees whose "hidden" skills and abilities might suit them better for a completely different task in another department (cf. Reihlen 1998, p.10f). The view of the departmental head would be that such a move would lead to his or her "losing" the employee involved.

A third point of criticism is that project managers and departmental heads are simply not up to the task of helping to further their employees' skills and abilities and promote their personal development – almost as an afterthought – in addition to pursuing the financial and functional project goals as best they can.

A last criticism would be the not insignificant danger that high potentials can be crushed by the hierarchy, or kept underfoot, since they represent a possible threat for the current "incumbent."

All four of these criticisms are highly problematic for companies operating in a highly-dynamic competitive environment. After all, the specialist and social skills of its employees are what decides a company's potential for success. Accordingly, the systematic development of competence should be a fundamental activity in any company.

The CoreMedia Competence Centers were brought into being for this precise reason: they serve the single purpose of expanding the skills and abilities of the company as necessary through internal development and acquisition. All members of staff receive professional support from the CCC for their own personal development. In the process, encouraging employees to take responsibility for their own development has proven useful: instead of being handed prizes from "on high," they are strongly supported in their own efforts to reflect personally on their current situation, to develop individual learning programs, and then to put these into action. The CCCs have proven to be a highly efficient tool for change management. Innovations on several different levels have systematically created free spaces for action:

All employees have the freedom to invest one day a month in topics in which they are interested. For this purpose, staff generally form what's known as "Peer Groups," in which they work on their chosen topics together with like-minded colleagues. The motivation for tackling the particular subject and the Peer Group's results are made available to all other employees over the intranet.

Every three months a one-day CCC Workshop is held (originally three workshops, each for one third of the workforce), to which all employees are invited. The CCC Workshops are the real highlight of self-organization *par excellence*. In the course of these Open Space Workshops, staff work entirely self-organized on tasks that they choose and define for themselves. Participants in workshops now include customers, partners, former colleagues, artists, journalists, supervisory board members, shareholders, and associates.

Every two weeks, individual staff members or entire peer groups have the chance to present their ideas internally to the company at what's known as a „Waterhole Meeting"; it's a chance to discuss issues with colleagues and management and to acquire some useful feedback. The best ideas have the chance of being actually implemented and thus compete for their share of the necessary resources.

All employees are regularly offered the chance of supportive interviews to assist in their chosen personal development path. These discussions offer staff feedback and coaching from experts in personnel development on the personal learning plans that they have themselves created.

Targeted personnel marketing is used by the CCC to constantly recruit new members of staff with the desired skills and abilities. This process makes deliberate use of the networks maintained by existing staff to identify both quality and shared values.

The CCC Workshops have in particular proven to be a very valuable foundation for our Enterprise 2.0 activities. After a few initial learning cycles, a pattern for success emerged that has now proven its value time and time again.

On the advantage of weak ties

Following a few less satisfactory experiences with workshops more strongly structured in advance, a CCC Workshop is now organized entirely as an "open space." By dispensing with set goals concerning content, tasks, team membership, or methodology, something very special can be achieved. All participants can and must decide for themselves what they will contribute and which topics they will support and dedicate themselves to. To relax the initial tension that naturally occurs with 100 participants in a single room and to elegantly introduce the main topic as quickly as possible, a small structural element has proven highly useful: the systematic creation of new contacts.

To break the ice, each participant seeks out an interview partner he or she doesn't yet know and interviews that partner on the day's main topic. What are the other person's thoughts on the topic, what are his or her personal experiences with it, and what expectations does he or she have for the event? In conclusion, the two interview partners then swap roles and re-interview themselves. Every ten minutes, the essence of the interview is written down on a postcard and posted on a large pinboard for all to see. The effect of this method of setting the mood is truly remarkable. Temporarily – i.e., for the upcoming workshop – it creates the "open space" referred to above. After the interview session, all participants are much more relaxed and less nervous than before. They are both interested in the main topic and open for new activities.

However, the real value in this exercise stems from its long-term effects. The search for an interview partner – one who is a stranger or one the participant barely knows – creates a particularly worthwhile kind of meeting: each interview not only promotes understanding but also creates a new node in the network. Put another way: many *weak ties* come into existence.[10] For example: for ten minutes, a software expert has the chance to see the world as a marketing professional sees it. At the end of those ten minutes, he or she can then experience the novelty of having the full attention of this marketing professional – and often even make him- or herself understood in the process. This creates understanding, contact, and trust that transcend the traditional departmental boundaries. The effects of these regular twenty-minute investments on our innovative ability, our speed of implementation and our creativity are fundamental for the entire company. If I had to decide on a single catalyst that I would be permitted to apply to my company every quarter, then it would be the chance to interview and be interviewed for ten minutes by an unknown colleague.

Networking and awareness, not structure and process

And now the actual Open Space can begin. Encouraged by the interviews, many varied topics are now thrown into the ring. Group formation, the organization of work, and the coordination between the teams is unproblematic, given the principle of self-organization. All of this just happens.

While many participants at their first Open Space still behave quite traditionally, remaining true to their original topic, movement between the teams increases in fluidity as time goes on. Our current Open Spaces are thus much livelier than in the past. As participants ourselves, we needed to learn how to handle our freedom, and we had to break a few taboos along the way as well. Today it's entirely acceptable practice to briefly join a group, consider its subject, comment or contribute an idea or two, and then move on to the next team.

After about four hours, each group then presents its results, briefly and succinctly, to the whole circle of participants. After receiving feedback, a *vernissage* (a.k.a. "poster session") follows, where all participants can discuss the results with their colleagues in more detail. In the process, participants also like to use an "offline" blog, pinning their comments on cards directly to the pinboard showing the group's results. The Open Space finishes with a closing reflection.

The CCC Workshops were an immediate success in bringing the company together and stimulating its creativity. However, one of the most important insights first came to light about six months later. The first Open Space Workshop generated about twenty recommendations from the total assembled workforce. And naturally, that same workforce promptly raised the question of what was now going to happen to all these excellent ideas. Indeed, the question itself stemmed from a healthy skepticism about whether these ideas would ever be developed further and actually put into practice. It was true: we hadn't defined a dedicated process for working further on the results. It had in truth seemed impossible to simply issue a management decree that would organize the necessary planning, resource allocation, and implementation – alongside all our other projects. As it was, we didn't even attempt it.

And, looking back, this decision was the best decision that we could have possibly made. A mere six months later, while preparing the next CCC Workshop, we reviewed our past achievements and – much to our amazement and surprise – found that the majority of the topics previously addressed had either already been implemented, or become an official project, or found their way into another subject area and were currently undergoing development there. The handful of ideas that had not yet been pursued were either clearly outside the company scope or were not yet mature enough to be put into practice.

My core insight from this experience was that we clearly needed neither a formal process nor a specific formal decision from a particular level of management to effectively and efficiently develop topics that were important to us. The single critical requirement was that the staff be given the necessary freedom to act so they could implement the insights from the CCC Workshops on their own.

My explanation for this phenomenon is thus the combination of collective awareness and individual freedom of action. The CCC Workshop created a collective awareness of the current topics facing the company as a whole. A kind of collective goal-finding process takes place. Each staff member decides which topics are relevant for CoreMedia, and which are not. Additionally, there is the certainty that all other employees have been through the same experience. Then, the same freedom to act granted on other occasions is used by staff to realize these ideas – self-organized and with impressive commitment.

I seriously doubt whether similar results would be obtained using rigid processes and hierarchical organizational structures. It is structure and process that tend to embody the problem and not the solution when the task is reacting to environmental changes. The key factors for the rapid discovery and realization of our insights were in my opinion as follows:

A high degree of **networking** among staff members;

An **awareness** shared by the entire group that others consider a particular topic to be an important topic for the company and that various aspects thus need to be considered;

Freedom to act – to realize and implement one's own insights "on company time";

Trust in one's environment and one's peers, knowing that one can and must make mistakes on the path to innovation.

It is worth noting at this point that the entire process initially took place almost entirely without any support from Web 2.0 tools such as blogs, wikis, forums, and other social software. All four patterns for success can be effectively implemented without any (digital) social media. In fact, I would go so far as to say that the introduction of digital media will not in itself succeed in realizing these patterns, for the primary requirement is trust.

Openness creates trust

Trust is a delicate plant: it thrives in only a few places, and wilts at the first sign of adversity. Only in an environment characterized by honesty and integrity can one reasonably hope that a robust culture of trust will develop. For self-organized structures, their very ability to function depends on trust. We therefore needed to consider the question of how we could create significantly greater trust. Luckily, the solution was handed to us on a platter: openness.

We had indeed cultivated a culture of openness since the founding of the company. Once a month, the "CoreVadis" meeting was held, at which important topics and facts were openly discussed. All staff are invited. As well as dealing with turnover, costs, and profit, the discussions also cover our project pipeline, our liquidity, and a great many other topics, all of which are suggested by staff or by management. This culture of openness has been particularly useful in times of crisis. This was a good start, yet it was possible to take our openness to an even higher level:

All members of the management team now rate both their own and their colleagues' performance. This rating process is carried out in an open forum, with all staff being able to view the published results.

The monthly strategy meetings invite five delegates from the staff to participate in the meeting as a "Sounding Board." As observers, advisers, and equal members in the meeting, they reflect on and rate management performance and participate in working out recommended solutions. The process thus takes the entire management team discussion into the open.

Explicit permission is also given for any staff member – and hence also any strategy meeting participant – to blog about their experiences and insights on our intranet. No exception is made for the content of the strategy meetings. As long as no breach of confidentiality occurs, publication on the Internet is also permitted.

Staff members may also attend the management team's jour fixe, which takes place every Monday afternoon. Acting as observers, they acquire a deep insight into our work.

The effects of this vastly improved transparency are consistently positive. In many cases, staff members who took the opportunity to experience the management team working together under "real-world" conditions were surprised by the quality of these meetings and also the complexity of the topics under discussion. While all the steps taken to improve our openness have concluded positively, it is the Sounding Board that has proven to be a tool with a quality all its own.

The Sounding Board was itself a proverbial bolt from the blue. At one of our group meetings, the criticism was aired that certain management decisions had been taken behind closed doors – to which one staff member responded by asking whether participation in the monthly strategy meeting would be at all possible. We were delighted to take this recommendation to heart and we implemented it the very next week. Five staff members participated in the two-day management team strategy meeting as a Sounding Board. With preliminaries completed, the group takes on two roles for the meeting. The management team works together as a team on the allotted tasks. Typically, this takes the form of a roundtable. The five staff members plus the CEO/CFO monitor events as observers on the sidelines.

After a few hours, the management team then invites the Sounding Board to reflect on progress. Observers and observed then swap roles. In the staff members' final reflection process, they rate the result, the methods taken to achieve it, and the general conduct of the management team. During this reflection process, management staff are confined to the roles of listener and audience. CEO and CFO are likewise restricted. After about twenty minutes, the Sounding Board and CEO/CFO take up the observer role once again.

The consequences of these functional role changes are remarkable. All those present are able to process information very quickly. The entire system thus develops a palpable dynamism. Although (or even because) there is no direct dialogue between the staff members and the management team, the observers' feedback has a force that is immediate, achieving its effects without additional discussion. At the same time, the Sounding Board instantly learns about the impact of its feedback.

The principle of "learning faster by listening" has also proven its value within our project teams. Instead of a discussion, a "lightning session" is used, where all participants provide a short summary of their opinion on the matter. This process can often help to solve problems of misunderstanding and conflict, since everyone can give their opinion unchallenged while listening carefully to what others have to say.

The Sounding Board's great success is primarily a result of the short feedback loops that it actively implements. It's rare for a management team to experience staff feedback on management analysis and opinion of such quality and so immediately. In addition, this methodology also increases trust by strongly promoting openness. Feedback was thus the key to improved openness, clarity, and trust.

"Feedback is a gift," says my coach, noting that "other people inform you about something of which you were previously unaware – namely, their feelings about your behavior. This gives you a chance to identify your blind spots." In retrospect, daily life in our company had not been especially noted for its honest and open feedback. It was a taboo subject – this open discussion of conflicts, individual fears, and emotions within the group. There was an atmosphere of fear about feedback – as can so often be felt in companies and other social organizations. Only once we had broken this taboo and started to employ an open, honest, and appreciative feedback system as a new form of communication was the atmosphere itself able to change, and self-organization able to properly flourish. Today, most teams are capable of solving their conflicts constructively and without outside help, and are thus able to regulate the group atmosphere. Immediate feedback from the environment replaces the old power structures and control systems.

Where prior control systems previously clung to a hierarchy, Enterprise 2.0 progressively replaces them with feedback loops as a basic conceptual unit. Things that used to (have to) be controlled from above are now self-regulated via multiple feedback mechanisms. Participants in this self-organization process must shoulder the important task of guaranteeing both the existence and proper functioning of these feedback loops in order to make self-organization possible in the first place. Thomas Malone has identified (2004) two key structural patterns in addition to hierarchy: democracy and market. And we have also gained some excellent experience with democratic structures in Enterprise 2.0.

"Take the lead!"

Mid-2005, we already had a good idea of the new process-oriented project structures that were designed to replace the rigid departmentalization, and we were thus now looking to establish our new management team. Not a single one of the previous management positions was retained. Generally, the selection of management personnel is a tricky business. Those who consider themselves eligible and harbor aspirations for career advancement, but who are not given the chance, often tend to react with open or barely-concealed hostility or, indeed, simply leave the company.

We wanted to take a fresh look and decided to let those most immediately affected by the selection process manage it themselves. So, we invited every staff member who was involved in any kind of management activity at CoreMedia to attend, and who would thus be a potential candidate for the ten management positions available. All of our departmental heads, our team leaders, key account managers and other management personnel met for a two-day workshop. The goal of the workshop was to find the right person for the right job.

The CFO and I took on the role of coach and adviser for the workshop, changing roles as appropriate. We had prepared an agenda that we were certain would lead us confidently to our common goal. First of all, the main group of thirty participants was given some structure. The end result was six smaller groups, generated via self-organization, each of whom could then contribute to a "Fish Bowl". This Fish Bowl consisted of a circle of twenty-four participants on the outside, with a smaller circle of six delegates in the center – i.e., one delegate from each smaller group.

Those present in the inner circle were thus guaranteed a high level of openness and clarity for the ensuing discussion and indeed for the entire decision-making process. All outer circle members were permitted to "recall" their delegate and then take his or her place in the discussion. The outer circle also had the possibility of using applause or disparaging comments to attempt to influence the inner discussion process.

The first task at hand was the standardization of the competence model for CoreMedia management personnel. Each member of management was supposed to posses the following skills and abilities: people skills, project management ability, strengths in the four balanced scorecard perspectives (finance, customers, processes, potential), and lastly the ability to integrate a variety of perspectives into a general overview – a skill that we designated as strategic competence.

Instead of taking the tedious option of writing a formal definition of all seven competence profiles – that we could all agree on   we took another route. We left it up to the main group and the Fish Bowl to agree on and name one or more shining examples of each competence profile at CoreMedia. In so doing, the group had to answer questions such as "Who has the best people skills?", or "Which of us is the best project manager?"

It worked. Within around thirty minutes, our competence profiles were standardized. Each profile now had one or two "best practice" examples, whose current competence level was now our common benchmark.

It was also a relief to be able to break a long-standing taboo. For the first time, team members were now able to talk openly about their own skills and abilities as well as about the differences that could be observed. Once the competence profile for each management position had been established, those present could now announce their intention to "run for office" – well aware of the fact that they would subsequently undergo both self-analysis and assessment by the group. In total, twenty-eight of the thirty participants announced their candidacy. They once more divided up into six groups and carried out self-analysis and group assessment on the basis of the competence model.

The initial deliberation for all candidates was: "If I consider myself to be as good a project manager as the best project manager at CoreMedia, I'll award myself five points. If on the other hand, I'm not a good candidate in this respect, I get only one point." Each candidate then asked for feedback from his or her own group of colleagues, ultimately agreeing on a common opinion, which was then documented by using a flipchart. This flipchart then made its way through the other five groups, who also contributed their group assessment of the candidates – although this time without the candidates present.

Initially, a palpable reserve could be felt in the teams, with few wanting to express criticism openly. However, this atmosphere soon thawed, giving way to a refreshingly direct and honest discussion. The collective awareness about the key skills and abilities needed to be developed rapidly, with the process also bringing to light a number of old and previously unresolved conflicts. The group discussions were characterized by deep honesty and appreciation, since both positive and negative aspects were considered equally, instead of mingling the two until both were no longer recognizable. The CFO and I also used the opportunity to avail ourselves of honest feedback from colleagues.

At the start of the next day, the participants in the Fish Bowl dedicated themselves to the staff members who had received ratings from their colleagues that were wildly different to their own, or who felt unfairly judged and wanted clarification of the results. These preparations marked the second stage of the workshop. Everyone involved now had a better understanding of the skills and abilities present within the team. These insights could now be used to develop recommendations about the staff members or teams that might best be suited for management responsibility.

The groups then presented their ideas in a *vernissage*. The results of this presentation were both surprising and unsettling: five of the six groups had shown absolutely no creativity at all regarding a key characteristic of the future management team. Quite the opposite: all of their recommendations suggested the same management duo, consisting of the most senior technical managers from the old structure – even though both of these individuals had had their conflicts in the past and had rarely bothered to try and work well together. The managers' competence profiles also failed to complement each other at all. I was surprised at how the group had chosen to restrict the selection potential in such a blinkered way. It seemed rather as if the previous management staff would retain power – and less like an alternative solution for the company.

Here it is also worth mentioning the fact that this phase saw the pair of strongest individuals cooperating with each other in order to ensure they didn't lose too much power in the impending management shake-up. One of these managers outlined the very same solution to me before the workshop – although I didn't take it seriously at the time. The majority of those involved viewed the imminent changes with some skepticism and seemed to feel that they weren't in a position to question the solution preferred by "those in charge." In fact, it was only possible to break this old power structure once my CFO and I took pains to clarify the future criteria for the establishment of the management team, underlining the fact that the structure had to be both balanced and sustainable. Finally, creativity could flourish and clear the way for a wealth of new solutions. Looking back, the participants themselves were unable to explain why they had initially refused to deviate from the first suggested solution. However, they did report that this decision had generated a feeling of fear and tension. Relief came only when the recommendation was ultimately questioned by myself and the CFO.

For me, this experience was an object lesson regarding decision-making within a group. The feeling of autonomy is instrumental for those participating in a change process. Only if a group contains individuals acting autonomously can one be sure that the potential domination of a group by a few of its members will be effectively countered.

Now it came to the crunch. The last task of the Fish Bowl was to agree on one or more recommendations for the make-up of the future management team and to present these to myself and the CFO. The group would advise us both, and we would then make the final decision. The scenario was as follows: ten positions were to be filled by the thirty employees present. The idea was that the group make this decision entirely autonomously. Accordingly, no guidelines were given as to the methodology. Decisions about time were also left to the group. Neither the CFO, the coach, nor I took any part in the decision-making process.

It took three and a half hours for the group to make its decision. We were then allowed back into the conference room. The group presented us their result: on the wall hung a single recommendation, unanimously accepted by all thirty participants. Nine of the ten positions were occupied. The tenth position was to be filled with an external candidate, stated the group, since the necessary specialist expertise was not present in the current company. This decision is in itself remarkable, since the group also contained participants who had themselves run for the positions on offer. The decision behind the recommendations was nonetheless unanimous.

While the recommended make-up for new management team matched my own expectations and those of my CFO in many instances, there were some surprises. Two engineers, whose interests, skills, and abilities had been previously unknown to us, had used the opportunity to successfully campaign for new areas of responsibility. The CFO and I took about three minutes to make our decision. We accepted the recommendations without exception. CoreMedia now had a new management team – and one that could count on broad-based support right from day one.

In the following six months, the new management team would replace the old departmental structure and usher in our new, more dynamic organization.

Love it, change it or leave it

The breakdown of the old power structures and the greater emphasis placed on the values of openness, readiness to learn, and self-organization did not go down well with all our employees. As with many change situations, there was initial apprehension and resistance – factors that we unfortunately made worse on occasion by failing to introduce new ideas as well as we could have. It took a while before the mood changed, helped by everyone working together constructively. But the time came when the majority of the staff accepted their new-found freedom – and some were even delighted by it. Yet not everyone shared this point of view. Some employees no longer wished to stay with the company under the new conditions. As could be expected, the staff turnover rose significantly in the next few months. It began with the management team itself, as the manager who had lost the most authority in the restructuring decided to leave the company. Others followed. The company itself also decided – by mutual agreement – to separate itself from a number of employees once it became clear that further collaboration made no sense for either party. On the other hand, there were a great many employees who overcame their initial skepticism and learned to love the new corporate culture. Many also contributed ideas, actively involving themselves in rectifying weak spots they had identified.

One and a half years after the disbanding of our departments, our dynamic force, collective awareness, and corporate unity had attained a level of quality that we hadn't been able to regain since the start-up phase of a company. At the same time, our capacity to learn and change has increased by leaps and bounds. Our process of continual change is, however, not yet over – in fact, quite the opposite, as our slogan "CoreMedia Evolution" makes very clear. It is an ongoing, permanent task, whose fundamental dynamic force is still increasing.

Further improvements to our self-organization and decentralized collaboration are in the pipeline. Our process-oriented structures have also proven a little constraining in a few areas. We are increasingly considering loose, cross-border organizations. A further trend toward dynamic, project-oriented organizational structures is thus conceivable. A dynamic leadership model, as has been in use at W.L. Gore for 50 years now, could well be the answer.

Since the introduction of the new organizational structure, it has been adjusted a number of times due to weaknesses that have been become apparent. One example is dual leadership, a strategy that was reconsidered after critical feedback from the staff and reflection within the management team. To solve problems of accountability and increase the speed of decision-making, each dual leadership duo chose one of the two of them to be the sole spokesperson for the following six months. So, finding the right balance between dependable organizational structures and dynamism is a constant challenge.

A cornerstone for the success of self-organization at CoreMedia is the public dialogue at our CCC Workshops, which supply a forum for the resolution of contentious questions while creating awareness for the new corporate culture. To accelerate and follow up on this dialogue, we also utilize our company-wide blog and dialogue platform, which lets all staff members open a discussion, comment on entries made by other employees, and rate or tag platform content. The dialogue is conducted entirely openly and has the power to generate a common awareness on important topics in a remarkably short period of time. Since all postings and comments can also be found in the personal blogs of each staff member, all those involved are noticeably careful about maintaining quality standards in their content. The number of reactions to a posting and its rating by individual colleagues has become an important benchmark for the relevance of the article. These factors are supplemented by interactive features, which allow one to search for recognized experts on a subject or identify colleagues whose articles or recommendations are similar to one's own.

The platform's attraction for employees, which became evident within only a few days, was also an expression of its innovative potential. Everyone has the chance to contribute original ideas and to clarify their position on a subject. A concentrated, innovative dialogue quickly ensues. By reflecting on the form the discussions take, it was possible to create awareness about the dialogue itself and the various roles taken within the dialogue. Feedback mechanisms also seemed decisive for improving the quality of the discussions held. Similar to the experience in a multi-user computer game, each point collected and each positive comment from colleagues creates a feeling of success that almost automatically leads to behavioral change. The appropriate selection of feedback loops for discussion is therefore a key design decision.

Markets inside and outside the company

Markets are also a form of discussion with one predominant feedback loop – price. The price allows participants in the market to gain feedback about the behavior of others involved in the market. Enterprise 2.0 also contains some strategies for market usage. CoreMedia is also currently involved in prototype testing of market mechanisms within the company. An important and recurrent coordination activity in every company is making decisions about the allocation of resources and priorities. In our daily business, continuous decision-making about prioritization is required, since companies will always have more opportunities than they have resources to handle them. In our decisions on resource allocation we have already achieved some excellent results by using self-organized team assignment. The next step will be to introduce an electronic marketplace for personnel resources. Instead of letting a horde of management staff regularly argue over resources in time-consuming discussions, we are currently reviewing a marketplace where sales teams can purchase the resources they need for their projects. The price is regulated by the demand for the specified experts. The contribution margin for project work at customers thus becomes comparable with the contribution margin that the same employee can achieve via a sales project. The efficiency of resource allocation and the value of the resource itself will thus presumably increase as a result of the increased transparency.

Market mechanisms are also being proposed as a solution to the prioritization of development projects. Via *decision markets*, which offer all employees the chance to value and trade the opportunities and risks of a number of different options, the collective estimation process is literally made visible. Clarity is similarly brought to the decision-making process. Ideally, the market price of the various options at any one point in time represents the collective knowledge of all those participating in the market. The total capital of the market participants is, in the medium-term, an appropriate indicator of the quality of their forecasts.

The wiki principle

In addition to hierarchies, democracies, and markets, there is a further mechanism for coordinating the activities of large groups: wikis. Following the example of Wikipedia, where hundreds of thousands of editors are collaborating on writing an encyclopedia , SYNAXON AG has documented its entire work guidelines and regulations in a wiki system. The regulations as presented in the wiki are the same for all. Yet each staff member is permitted to change these rules – at any time and without authorization – if he or she thinks that a regulation is wrong. Employees quickly come to develop a sense for situations where a change is best first discussed with their colleagues before being implemented.

At CoreMedia, criticism was reiterated about the lack of documentation about patterns for success with a proven track record. The proportion of ad hoc processes was presumably too great. Yet the danger of suffocating bureaucracy and associated rigidity spoke against the introduction of compulsory process models. The introduction of a wiki in the manner pursued by SYNAXON AG presents a useful way to solve the paradox presented by Enterprise 2.0: structures need to be helpful on the one hand, yet retain their versatility on the other.

Where networks flourish, boundaries blur

Reviewing the last few years, we can say that increased networking also blurs the boundaries between departments and the levels within hierarchies. The boundaries between different teams, different areas of responsibility, work and private life, companies and their environment, and even between markets and their subject areas are much more porous than they were before. The visible effects at CoreMedia are the targeted usage of creative potential, increased dynamism and versatility, as well as a pronounced atmosphere of trust among our colleagues. Today, we can see a great many more positive characteristics than negative ones, whose effects are of course felt in the corporate culture as a whole. The company has experienced a highly fruitful discussion about and reflection on our values and the purpose of the company. What do we stand for, and what connects us all? With an increased awareness for these questions and the answers we had provided for them as a group, it was only natural that the relationship of staff to the company would take on a new direction.

Instead of presenting our employees with pre-fabricated messages and controlling the communication with the public, we adopted a different strategy. We motivated our staff to tell their own, individual stories, bringing their convictions to a wider audience – both internally and externally. This participation in internal dialogue and the strong collective awareness that it generated was also responsible for creating equally authentic and coherent external communication. Individual personalities are given far greater room to flourish. And yet, instead of a cacophony, a pleasant concert of many individual voices is the result.

And that's what it's all about.

WORKS CITED

Krönung, Hans-Dieter (2007): Die Management-Illusion. Warum Erfolg nicht kopierbar ist und was Manager daraus lernen sollten. Stuttgart.

Thomas Malone (2004): The Future of Work: How the New Order of Business Will Shape Your Organization, Your Management Style, and Your Life. Boston, Mass.

Reihlen, Markus (1996): Die Heterarchie als postbürokratisches Organisationsmodell der Zukunft? Arbeitsbericht Nr. 96. Seminar für Allgemeine Betriebwirtschaftslehre, Universität Köln.

David Weinberger
The Risk of Control

There is a good reason why Web 2.0 is notoriously difficult to define: the term arose not from a definition but from a white board full of diverse examples. Tim O'Reilly, the publisher of technology books, and his friends listed everything they could think of that had changed in the past few years, from Wikipedia to blogs to Google Maps. The items had in common only that they were significantly different from what came before them. They seemed to fall into a couple of rough clusters: the rise of user voices and the interoperability of applications and data. Later, O'Reilly would point to the "network effect" – the fact that having lots of people connected brings about unpredictable results – as central to all of Web 2.0. But it turns out that there is one factor that runs throughout the loosely-bound set of Web 2.0 applications: they all show the price we've paid for trying to reduce risk by increasing control.

The case for control is simple, and in fact primitive. We try to affect our environment in ways that will benefit us. Control lowers risk, whether it's the risk of being eaten by saber-tooth tigers or having our market capitalization drop. Control in turn rests on predictability. We anticipate the regularities in nature to avoid the dangers we cannot control, and we build regularities into our institutions to make them predictable. Either way, we use control to avoid risk.

Control is at the heart of business. And of course Enterprise 2.0 does not give up all control. Not at all. Nevertheless, Enterprise 2.0 can only be understood within the framework of changes in control, because that's the thread running through Web 2.0. User-generated content such as blogs matter not simply because lots of people are writing them, but because they're being written by people who are not being centrally managed or controlled. Application interoperability matters because it allows developers to use services created by others without asking for permission; the work of one person's hands enhances the work of another, all without having to clear it with anyone first. And network effects themselves occur only when the network reaches a size and complexity sufficient to make it unpredictable and thus essentially uncontrollable.

This is no surprise since the Web itself succeeded because it systematically excluded control structures from its architecture. Anyone can link to anything. Anyone can post whatever page they want. Anyone can visit any page they want. The Web was able to scale only because it was permission-free. Further, to institute a system of control, the Web would have had to centralize itself. That central point would make the system less robust, for if it failed, the Web itself would fail. More important, a centralized control point for managing access would have almost inevitably created an authority subject to the implicit and explicit forces favoring tradition and the status quo. The Web and the Internet are the greatest scenes of innovation in human history because they are uncontrolled.

Of course, the Web is not entirely uncontrolled. What is posted there is subject to local laws: libel someone in a Web post and you are as likely to be sued as if you libeled someone in print. Access to the Internet is itself controlled in various ways, from terms and conditions spelled out by the organizations that provide Internet access to laws requiring the use of national identity numbers in some countries. So, the Web and the Internet embrace a mix of risk and control, just as every business organization does. The online infrastructure has opted for very little control while accepting a large amount of risk. The risks are serious, threatening the operation of the network itself, making available material that may be harmful (child pornography, instructions on how to build bombs), and raising the very real possibility that so much material will come online that people won't be able to find what is of genuine value. Yet the rewards have been substantial, including a rapid increase in available knowledge, the ability to coordinate across multiple divides, and a free field for rapid innovation (including, as Clay Shirky (2007)[11] points out, lowering the cost of failure). These are advantages most enterprises deeply desire.

Enterprises are not the Web. Even the most enthusiastic Enterprise 2.0 is still mainly an enterprise and only somewhat 2.0. Businesses cannot simply wish away the government regulations that constrain them. Nor can they go from multi-tiered hierarchies to flat pools of miscellanized workers. The Quality Control group is still going to exert control over quality. Ethical codes are going to continue to restrain bad behavior, or at least we hope they do. Enterprise 2.0 does not do away with all control. Nevertheless, what makes it 2.0 is, to a large degree, how much control it cedes.

We can see this most all of in the enterprise itself:

Markets. Traditional companies have assumed that they can control their customers by selectively releasing information. You would only show photos of your products in perfect condition. You would only describe your products' strengths. If you made boots that were designed to withstand mud but not water, you would tout them as perfect for gardening after the rain, but would neglect to mention that if you step in a puddle, your feet are going to be soaked. Companies hoped thereby to control their customers' behavior and called it "marketing."

From the very first, however, the Web has put customers in touch with other customers. If you want to know if, say, a piece of exercise equipment is worth the money, you'll Google it. You'll find the information from the company, but you'll also find customers talking about it. If the equipment works well for eight months but then tends to develop squeaks, or if it's great so long as you're at least of moderate height, the networked market will know it. Networked markets are almost always more knowledgeable than the companies they're talking about because when customers talk, they're not blinded by self interest. Also, customers discover facts about products that are so context-specific that companies may not even know them. Perhaps a particular Wi-Fi router stops working whenever a microwave oven is turned on, or perhaps it causes a smoke alarm to whine. The manufacturer can't foresee every interaction because life is more complex than any conceivable testing lab. Further, there are often customers with deep expertise that they share in networked market conversations. Those conversations get very smart very fast.

Not only has marketing slipped out of the control of businesses, the attempt to re-exert control over markets can have quite a negative effect. A company that surreptitiously pays bloggers to say nice things about its products will look manipulative and ethically shady when that fact emerges. There's also a risk in trying to look hip and webby without actually making any changes. A company can seem like a middle-aged father dressing like his teen-aged kids and using their lingo. It's just embarrassing.

On the other hand, if a company is willing to give up on trying to keep the market conversations relentlessly positive, if they're willing to enter into those conversations as people who acknowledge their vested interests, but who have some genuine passion for their products, they can benefit greatly from the growth of networked markets. It's not easy to do. Companies are so used to trying to control their markets that they often enter into the new market conversations with the aim of subverting them. That will hurt the brand. The first rule for an enterprise that's trying to be 2.0 is: respect the conversation. It belongs to your customers, not to you. Your customers would rather talk with one another than with you. You are not the center of the universe anymore, even when it comes to your own products.

The risk of giving up the attempt to control market conversations is worth it. By entering into those conversations appropriately, companies learn what their customers really think, they can build person-to-person loyalty, they build a trusted channel of communication in case of crisis, and they increase the value of their brand. The risk of *not* giving up some measure of control over markets is that your company will become a black hole. If you're not willing to talk in an interesting – and that means uncontrolled – way, then no one will listen to you. No one wants to hear a company spout its old marketing slogans. Going dark in the market is a terrible risk to take.

Management. The typical hierarchical organization, modeled on the Roman army, is a system not only of control but of power. This is so deeply ingrained that it is hard to see how existing companies will be able to get much past it. The decision system mirrors the accountability system mirrors the social system mirrors the incentive system, and they all mirror a pyramid. Even the physical layout of the office place usually reflects the hierarchical topology of the organization.

For some types of projects, that's exactly what we need. No one suggests that we could build a skyscraper by using the principles that enabled strangers to build an online encyclopedia. Even though skyscrapers are in the literal sense built bottom-up, building them takes top-down management. But even within projects as structured as building a skyscraper, there are elements of non-hierarchical organization. The teams working together are probably less motivated by the command and control structure than by their feelings for one another and their pride in what they're building. Within this niche, management may look more like Wikipedia's than General Electric's.

But the most important effect of Web 2.0 on management will be what is to come as our workforce fills with people who take for granted that they don't need management, and if they do, they'll figure out for themselves how to do it. To them, the permanent structure of the enterprise looks like an encrusted form that is unlikely to be responsive to the real needs of the project. Just-in-time, do-it-yourself management seems to them to be much more rational, efficient, and humane. Attempts by traditional leaders to exhibit the traits of leadership will often strike this new generation as negative: an unrealistic attempt to control what is best left uncontrolled, a pathetic effort to retain one's power, a ridiculous attempt to puff oneself up.

Time. Perhaps the most pervasive change in control is also the hardest to talk about. Businesses have tried to control just about every aspect of time. People punch time clocks, or at least are expected to show up during working hours. Processes are timed and time-lined. Reports are due at precise intervals. Meetings recur with predictable frequency. Products and careers have lifecycles. Modern corporate life could be understood almost entirely by how it controls time.

Web 2.0 de-structures time. Just ask anyone in the media. Newspapers were used to printing once a day. Online, news sites have to be as continuous as the news itself. Likewise, broadcasters used to have to lay their programming out into a timeline. Miss the broadcast and you've missed the bus. Now the audience expects to be able to watch on its schedule, and it will make that happen whether the broadcaster wants it to or not.

Enterprise 2.0 is likewise characterized by how it de-structures time. How much control over schedules will it retain and how much will it let its customers, partners, and employees have? The balance in each case will emerge as businesses figure out which sort of time works in which circumstances. For example, many companies have already discovered that letting people work at home can make them more productive. Similarly, asynchronous communication media such as e-mail and semi-synchronous media such as instant messaging are replacing some of the highly synchronized events such as weekly meetings. Why meet once a week when workers can achieve continuous partial meetings (to play on Linda Stone's phrase "continuous partial attention"[12]) via e-mail, blogs, Twitter, instant messaging, chat, and social networking sites?

The corporate de-regulation of time looks inefficient to some companies. They are fighting the incursion of personal time into on-site workdays by monitoring Internet usage. Woe betide the employee who shops online during work! Yet others are willing to trust their employees enough to manage their own time; the interpenetration of work time and personal time is one of the continuing stories over the past decade or so.

Even the change in how workers dress is due in part to the de-regulation of corporate time. Entering an office in the morning used to be like a rapid change in seasons, requiring a change in clothing. But as personal time interpenetrates work time, having to dress up to go to work seems constricting, inefficient, and symbolic of an apartness that does not characterize Enterprise 2.0.

In all three of these areas – marketing, management, and time – there are risks to giving up control. But there are also risks to maintaining control where it is not needed. Clamping down carries five basic risks.

First, control can introduce inefficiencies. This can be as evident as having to fill out forms to certify that processes have been completed or as subtle as habituating workers to steps that may have no real value. Of course, sometimes the extra work required to control a process may have crucial benefits. Enterprise 2.0 looks at these processes with a fresh eye.

Second, even the attempt to control workers through traditional extrinsic means such as pay and discipline can be de-moralizing to Enterprise 2.0 employees. They may not be motivated purely by love of the project, but Enterprise 2.0 workers presumably feel some of the kinship and passion found in collaborative projects on the Web.

Third, over-controlling a process can squeeze the innovation out of it. If employees are allowed to experiment and fail they may discover advances that were invisible to the old controlled environment. This is an argument in favor of *play*.

Fourth, over-controlled enterprises mask the natural expertise of their workers, and even of their customers. For example, while blogging at work might look like a waste of company time, blogs also often surface competencies that otherwise would go unnoticed. Perhaps there's a marketing writer who also happens to know a lot about which video cards are best for games, and perhaps that information will turn out to be crucial to the company. Keeping those competencies hidden deprives the company of a valuable asset already in its midst.

Fifth, over-control is unrealistic. Because control is based on fear, it often takes on the properties of magic and superstition, as if repeatedly doing things the same way is an amulet against risk. Collaborative projects on the Web, and Enterprise 2.0 at its best, shape themselves around the needs of the project. They don't start out with a set of positions to be filled. Rather, people respond to the demands of the work itself. This makes them far more responsive because they are in closer touch with the complexity of how things are, rather than the simplicity control demands.

Enterprise 2.0 is not out of control. Rather, it is in control just enough, for Enterprise 2.0 recognizes that while control manages risk, control also carries its own risks.

Ralf Reichwald, Kathrin Möslein, Frank Piller
Creating Value Interactively - Challenges for Company Management

Introduction

The vision of open structures for enterprise and management that one finds at the heart of the objectives set by Enterprise 2.0 relies on self-organization and collaboration in the value creation process. It requires that companies not only remove their intra-organizational barriers, but also those obstructing the company's interactions with its customers. Within a company, this breaking down of walls is characterized by the partial relinquishment of hierarchical mechanisms for coordination and the "art of letting go." However, the cooperative process of interactive exchange and value creation cannot simply be restricted to the internal workforce and prevented from ever leaving the company premises. The vision is instead far-sighted, seeking the inclusion of external parties, customers, and value chain partners in the interactive process. Competence in interaction on the part of both the employees and the customers of a company thus form the key to a successful cross-border process of interactive value creation. The novelty of this form of interaction, together with its intensity, presents management unique challenges. This paper will focus on both of these issues. We will first turn to consider the basic precepts of 'interactive value creation' (Section 2), showing how a path can be traced from the traditional and dominant organizational forms – 'hierarchy and market' – to interactive value creation (Section 3). Section 4 introduces the principle of openness: the idea of "commons-based peer production." Section 5 uses case studies to illustrate principle and implementation. Yet how can companies, their management, staff, and customers master the central challenge of competence in interaction? This is addressed by Section 6, ensuring that the chances – and also the limitations – of interactive value creation are not surmised prematurely. This is also an articulation of the opportunities and limitations of the vision of Enterprise 2.0.

What is interactive value creation?

Interactive value creation is cooperation coupled with social exchange. The principle of interactive value creation necessitates a strongly co-operative process. At the core of this process lie the strategies of the company itself, which no longer sees its customers or users as passive recipients and consumers at the end of a value creation process wholly owned by the manufacturer. Instead, users are often full partners in the value chain, working with companies or other users to help design products or services, advising on – or even assuming responsibility for – their development and production. This active role played by both employee and customer transforms the company-dominated value creation model into an interactive process of value creation (Reich-wald/Piller 2006).[13]

Interactive value creation takes place when a company or other insti-tution contracts out a task previously carried out by the internal work-force to a large, unspecified network of customers and users, in the form of an open call for participation. An 'open call' is understood to mean that the task to be completed is publicly announced, with exter-nal problem-solvers deciding their participation via self-selection. In many cases, the completion of the task will be carried out as a collabo-rative act between multiple users; other cases will involve only a single agent. The task itself may involve innovation (creation of new know-ledge) or it may require operative involvement (such as participation in a marketing campaign or helping out with product configuration). In each scenario, however, the active role assumed by customers and users transforms the company-dominated value creation process into one of mutual co-creation.

A real-world example of what we mean by interactive value creation is provided by the company Threadless. The company, founded in Chicago in 2000, has achieved great success by selling what is in fact a relatively simple product: printed t-shirts. Nonetheless, the two founders and their twenty or so employees are now turning a profit of nearly half a million dollars a month – all this with a minimal workforce and zero development risk (Ogawa/Piller 2006). This success can be attributed to the outsourcing of all essential value creation activities to the customers, who greet this decision with unbounded enthusiasm.[14] Some users create new designs for t-shirts and upload them on to the company Web site. Around 800 new designs per week are uploaded in this way. Most users of course neither have the time nor the inclination (nor indeed the ability) to create new designs themselves. Crucially, however, they are no longer simply traditional buyers, since they perform another key function within a fashion company – that of project management.

Every week, more than 200,000 users rate the new designs, while making recommendations for improving other available t-shirts. And Threadless takes these ratings at face value: every week, the company manufactures around four new designs – chosen exclusively from the designs that the majority of the users rated as especially impressive ("I love it," in Threadless-speak). These printed shirts are then mass-produced and sold for US$ 15 – an estimated 60,000 t-shirts every month. Customers even shoulder a large proportion of market risk for the company, since they (morally) commit themselves to buying their t-shirt of choice before this shirt is actually manufactured. This commitment is expressed by clicking a small button ("I'd buy it"): by clicking, the user not only expresses admiration for the design, but also indicates that he or she is a prospective buyer. In addition, the customers provide Threadless with advertising, offering both models and images for the catalog photos, while also recruiting new customers.

Yet the customers do not feel they are being exploited – quite the opposite, in fact. They are full of enthusiasm for a company that offers them the opportunity of participation. They not only protect Threadless from lookalike firms but supply a constant stream of ideas for improving the company and making it more productive. Threadless itself concentrates on the job of maintaining and improving the interaction platform that supports the communication between the company and its customers. The company defines the rules of play and manages the actual physical process (manufacturing and distribution). It also rewards its customer designers: each design that is selected for manufacture rewards its creator with a payment of US$ 2,000.

From hierarchy and market to interactive value creation

The Threadless example is more than just a creative gimmick. It is an entirely new way of coordinating value creation using the division of work. Division of work is the foundation on which our economy is built. The model leverages specialization effects while enabling the efficient handling of complex tasks. Simultaneously, however, this division of work incurs costs (transaction costs). As a result, economists have long sought ways of organizing processes involving work division efficiently. To date, there have been two main alternatives: hierarchical coordination within a company (creation of a good within a company) or the utilization of market forces involving supply and demand (purchase of a good on the open market). A mixed form is supplied by the various inter-company networks.

The concept of how companies create value that still prevails today can be traced back to principles that were first advanced over 100 years ago, in the then-burgeoning industrial society. Frederick Taylor's essay "Scientific Management" in particular, with its focus on lowering production costs, was so persuasive that it has influenced all further debate on the subject. In his model, the economic principle of rational choice, scarcity, and the problem of distribution characterize the business management issues faced in organization, the division of work, and the coordination of the value creation process (Gutenberg 1951; Kosiol 1959). The focus thereby is on the efficient execution of company-internal value creation processes. Porter's model (1985) of a value creation chain handed management theory an integrated approach for this value creation process, arguing that everything from development, production, and sales through to the delivery of goods and services could be organized and managed by using the productive factor of information. In the early 1990s, Hammer and Champy (1993) introduced their idea of business process re-engineering to acclaim in the business world. Their approach, which enjoyed widespread adoption, argued that by focusing on internal efficiency, one can create value in a company by widening the margin between the willingness to pay and the total sum of manufacturing costs.

This internal focus was later expanded to the vision of a company possessing no actual boundaries (thus potentially virtual), in which a closely-integrated network of professional agents work in concert within a harmonious value creation chain comprising many different organizations (Picot/Reichwald 1994; Picot/Reichwald/Wigand 2003). In the search for new, efficient value creation systems (supply chain management), the suppliers (and suppliers of the suppliers) themselves were now included in the process. Finally, with the advent of the Internet and its concomitant potential for lowering transaction costs, the interfaces to the consumer were also factored into calculations of economic efficiency (electronic commerce). However, each and every step along this path of development has been accompanied by the assumption that the ultimate source of economic value creation is the pursuit of (company- or network-) internal cost efficiency.

Yet customers and users do not generally acknowledge the internal operative efficiency of a supplier or network. While customers and users may enjoy the lower prices that result from this efficiency, studies have shown that the pursuit of ever-greater operative efficiency within a network will not provide a long-term, sustainable competitive advantage (Porter 1996). While operative efficiency is a necessary requirement for long-term competitive advantage, it is not a sufficient one. Current studies show instead that the company's structuring of interfaces to the outside world and the activities that take place on its periphery should be seriously considered when addressing the creation of value. This observation places an actor center-stage who has previously been largely ignored in the debate about the design of the value creation process: the customer and/or the user.

In the present day, we observe that customers not only consume the products of operational value creation, but also that they themselves make a significant contribution to the value creation process (Ramirez 1999). This contribution is not only made autonomously within the customer domain (an area that has long been a subject of study within microeconomics in relation to consumer production – see e.g., Becker 1965; Lancaster 1966), but also arises out of an interactive and cooperative process with both the manufacturers and the other users of a good. Within this process, customers and users help to extend the know-how, skills, and resources possessed by the manufacturer (Gibbert/Leibold/Probst 2002). Interactive value creation entails the integration of customers as a strategic factor within the manufacturer's operations so that they can produce value as part of an extended value creation network. It is crucial that this value is not assessed merely in terms of the simple increase in difference between the willingness to pay and internal efficiency. The primary aim here is the shared creation of innovation in relation to both products and processes.

The process involves the delegation of a task previously completed by the employees of a company (or within an enclosed network of well-defined partners) to an open, undefined and large group of agents located at the periphery of the company (Benkler 2002; Huff et al. 2006). This delegation process is initiated by an open call for participation. This is understood to mean that either the focal company or an agent within the network formulates a problem at the technical or organizational level ("Need a cool t-shirt design!", "How should I wash my t-shirt so the colors don't run?", "Who will swap their panda t-shirt for a Star Wars t-shirt?"), before publishing this statement on an openly-accessible platform. All potential agents then decide individually whether they will participate or not (self-selection). Often, the task will then be completed via collaboration between multiple users (peer production); in other cases, a single agent will complete the task alone. The novelty here is not simply the task allocation process (public offer and self-selection), however, but also the method applied to solve a complex task via the division of work.

Crucially, throughout the evolution of organizational methods for value creation via the division of work, it is not merely the perception of the agents actively involved in the value creation process that changes. Change is also seen in concepts addressing the best method of resolving the organizational problem, i.e., the coordination and motivation of the individual agents who carry out the task as a whole via the division of work:

Taylor's model emphasizes above all the use of hierarchical coordination and motivation via financial incentives, with these activities occurring in a closed value creation system.

Network theorists extend this conceptual structure to include a combination of market- and hierarchy-based coordination strategies, while also stressing the importance of non-monetary incentives.

Interactive value creation expands both of these classical coordination strategies (hierarchy and market) to include a third approach: self-selection and self-organization of tasks by (highly-) specialized agents, whose motivation is primarily the (personal) utilization of the goods created by the collective, although this participatory desire can be strengthened by a multitude of additional social, intrinsic, and extrinsic motives.

We can use our Threadless case study to examine these principles. In a traditional fashion company, the head of design would commission the best-qualified specialist to design a new t-shirt with a particular kind of motif. In the process, he or she would either select the staff member who was most suited for the design task, or would perhaps simply choose an employee who seemed to be the least snowed under with work at the time. Alternatively, a personal address book search might be made to find the external designer who would, in the opinion of the head of design, deliver the "best" design. In both cases, the design would be paid for at a fixed price. The head of design would set a delivery date to ensure that the entire production process for the product would not be endangered, and would then monitor the observation of this deadline. On delivery, he or she would accept the design, make suggestions for improving it or perhaps even reject it entirely ("That's not at all like the design agreed on in our briefing."). The head of design thus coordinates the division of work for value creation using methods of control derived from hierarchy or the market.

At Threadless, however, there are no heads of design who instruct their employees to design a specific prototype. Threadless simply invites anyone who feels so inclined to participate in solving the problem. External designers make decisions about their participation, the extent of their involvement in the solution, and which motif to use on an entirely autonomous basis. The traditional, hierarchical mechanisms of coordination are replaced by self-motivation, self-selection, and self-organization on the part of the agents. Hierarchies and traditional markets are absent. Everyone makes the best contribution that he or she is capable of. This comes especially to the fore when a participant is already in possession of knowledge that can be re-used to solve the problem at hand. Yet the Threadless model is not limited merely to the designers. It also includes the thousands of "normal" users who rate the new designs, advertise the products via affiliate marketing, and, naturally, actually buy the end products. Our studies of Threadless reveal that nearly all of the customers who buy a t-shirt have also previously rated other t-shirts. Once aggregated, the contributions made by the normal users have an equally important part to play in the efficient creation of value within the company.

Another shining example for peer production is Wikipedia, whose participants not only integrate new material into the system as a whole, but also amend and improve existing articles. All agents involved in the process make autonomous decisions about the tasks they accept and their level of participation. Wikipedia even outsources the key function of quality control, making it the collective responsibility of all contributors. The quality control mechanism itself is grounded in Wikipedia's value system.

It is even possible to use these principles to create highly-complex technical products – although a slightly different set of ground rules applies. A good example of this is provided by Innocentive, a US company running a paid broker service that works by bringing problems and problem solvers together. The business model for Innocentive (the company name is a fusion of "innovation" and "incentive") is simple: a business seeks a solution for a problem that its R&D department cannot solve alone. The business uploads a description of the problem – accompanied by formulae or diagrams as required – to the Innocentive Web site and names a monetary reward that is generally in the region of between US$ 10,000 and US$ 100,000. This reward money is presented to the problem solver who provides the best solution to the problem within a certain time frame (e.g., two months). More than 100,000 creative minds are currently registered with Innocentive, regularly scanning the newest postings. The client remains anonymous at all times, to protect company interests. For its services, the company requests a fee from those who post the problems. The innovation portal has seen rapid expansion since its launch in 2001. Originally a spin-off of the pharmaceutical giant Eli Lilly, today the portal can even count the competition among its customers – names such as BASF, Novartis, Nestlé, or the consumer products giant Procter & Gamble. This service also typifies a completely new way of organizing value creation: instead of handing over the task to a known "best" scientist (whether internal or external), the problem itself is made the subject of a public tender. Individuals make an autonomous decision to participate in finding a solution.

An assessment of Innocentive's success rate demonstrates the high efficiency of this kind of open system (Lakhani 2005): more than half of all problems posted were solved in a short period of time – even though internal staff had been unable to find a solution in many of these cases. Many problem solvers compete successfully because they are already aware of the solution. This demonstrates another key principle in interactive value creation: the efficient re-utilization of an available body of knowledge. Many winners already knew of a solution for a similar problem in another area and were able to transfer this solution across to the new field of study (for a description of the same mechanism in action regarding open source software, see Lakhani/von Hippel 2002). This process neatly hurdles a problem met in technical problem solving: the "local" search for solutions – the classic scenario where a company is able to search for a solution only in the fields of study that it is aware of, and where such solutions must also lie within the skill set of its own R&D staff. Innocentive removes the barriers of this "local" search – as indeed does Threadless, in comparison to the head of design at a traditional fashion company.

Preconditions for "commons-based peer production"

Yale scholar Yochai Benkler (2002, 2006) terms the organizational principle that informs the interactive value creation process "commons-based peer production": "peer production," since a group of similar individuals ("peers") work together to produce a good, and "commons-based," since the result is made available to the community and is based on freely-available ("common") knowledge. The idea of interactive value creation takes commons-based peer production as a foundation, extending this further to include a framework within which a focal company initiates, moderates, or supports this process – exactly as is the case with our examples of Threadless or Innocentive.

Three preconditions must, however, be fulfilled for interactive value creation to function properly:

First, the entire task at hand must be capable of being divided up into multiple sub-tasks ("granularity" principle), which are then distributed using an interaction platform. This is essential for lowering barriers to entry and reducing the amount of effort required from individual users. The aim is to resolve complex tasks by using the distributed abilities of a multitude of users, with each user making an optimal contribution of his or her personal expertise. Wikipedia provides a perfect example of this principle: while a single user could never hope to write the entire encyclopedia, the combined contributions of thousands of participants (working on minor tasks such as entering a keyword or correcting an error) can succeed in mastering a monumental task. In the case of Threadless, this is achieved by separating the participants into two groups: the "designers," who possess certain creative faculties, and the "raters," who are potential customers and need only consult their personal taste when making their decisions. With Innocentive, precisely-specified sub-problems are the rule (e.g., "develop a molecule with these characteristics"), enabling the allocation of the task to experts who are in possession of precisely the desired skill set.

Second, it must be possible to attract a sufficiently large number of motivated participants. The motivation shown by participating customers and users is one of the central aspects of interactive value creation. We recall the economic theory that agents act rationally, only contributing to the success of a project if they themselves receive something of value in return. Yet our sample companies sometimes supply no material incentives whatsoever. At Threadless, more than 800 designers upload new designs on to the site every week, while only three or four actually win anything. What motivates designers to participate here? One fact is of course the lure of the prize money: US$ 2,000 is a sum of money around four times larger than the typical fee paid for a t-shirt design at standard contractual rates. Another factor, however, is the chance to measure oneself against other users competitively while also showcasing one's personal design talents. One can appreciate that achieving a high profile in the market is no easy matter for (up-and-coming) graphic designers. Threadless offers such artists a platform for displaying their work, thereby enabling them to make potential future clients aware of their talent. Apart from these factors, designers also value feedback on their designs that they receive from users. Each t-shirt not only receives a rating, but is also allocated its own forum. Such forums may receive as many as ninety comments from users, ranging from simple complimentary notes to detailed analyses of the ways in which a t-shirt design could be improved on.

At Innocentive, the substantial prize money would seem to be the motivational factor at first glance. Yet a dissertation by Karim Lakhani (2005) from the Massachusetts Institute of Technology has shown that the participants are not only keen to win the prize money, but are also highly motivated by the competitive environment. They not only hope to turn their expertise into money, but also achieve satisfaction from the act of creativity itself, and in measuring themselves against scientists from all over the world.

A considerable corpus of research is now available on the subject of motivation among open source programmers, and it shows that where users are active, intrinsic motivation often prevails over the expectation of an extrinsic benefit (remuneration, use of the created solution). The intrinsic benefit is derived from working on the project for its own sake. An activity is valued on its own terms and is performed without expectation of any immediate service in return. Often, the interaction experience itself is seen as positive and beneficial if it can generate feelings of enjoyment, competence, discovery, and creativity

(Deci et al. 1999). Participation is also explained by the fulfillment of social norms. Examples of such norms include reciprocal behavior, public interest, and fairness.

The third precondition brings the actual benefit attainable with interactive value creation: openness and non-proprietary legal protection for the goods created ("commons-based"). Yet this is itself only partially fulfilled – if indeed at all – in our examples of Threadless and Innocentive. Only in cases where prior knowledge can be used to solve new problems without requiring complicated licensing procedures do we see real gains in efficiency from the new approach to the networked division of work. In its ideal form, interactive value creation thus requires the free publication of the knowledge created by participants, in a way enabling simple re-use, re-combination, and further development by other parties. Eric von Hippel (2005) thus views the existing patent systems as a serious obstacle that hinders the pursuit of innovation in a number of important areas. He advocates reforms that would simplify the re-use of existing bodies of knowledge.

Threadless and Innocentive on the other hand still operate within the traditional system of intellectual property rights. Problem solvers at Innocentive must prove that they own the intellectual property involved in a solution (ideally, by owning an existing patent) in order to be able to license this property to the problem owner on payment of the prize money. (Much of the work at Innocentive is involved with guaranteeing this exact same transfer.) Similarly, the remuneration paid to designers at Threadless includes the acquisition of the copyright for t-shirt printing.

These restrictions do not, however, apply to open source software. Here, an approach to a problem can be based in large part on available knowledge and may also include substantial portions of it within the new solution. This method is in the long term far more efficient than needing to clarify the exact property rights of each item of knowledge on an individual basis. However, this is not a suitable place for studying the subject in greater depth, and we wish only to point out the fundamental principles at work: while interactive value creation does work within traditional systems of property rights, it will only achieve its true power with the introduction of new, open models for rights and licensing.

Case studies for interactive value creation

Stata Corp. is a manufacturer of statistical software. The company takes a systematic approach to the interactive co-development of its products with its users and has adopted an appropriate middle course between open and proprietary frameworks with regard to the resultant end products. Customers (users) of the Stata package are primarily scientists or developers, who utilize the program to conduct a wide range of statistical tests. The software enables the simple programming of new tests in cases where the test applications offered by the program are unable to complete a specific task at an acceptable level (of sophistication). Stata has therefore split its software package into two parts. The first part, which is proprietary, provides core functionality and is developed by the company itself. It is not free and is sold under a traditional software licensing framework. The second part is open and incorporates significant contributions from the user community in the form of new statistical algorithms and tests. Stata provides support for these expert users in the form of a dedicated development environment and an online forum, where users can exchange tests they have written, ask questions, and make improvements to work developed by other users (von Hippel 2005).

However, since not every user will be an expert user, or a possess a sufficiently high level of programming expertise, Stata has developed a system that enables it to select the "best" or most popular user contributions on a regular basis with the aim of integrating them into the next official release of its software package. Decisions of this kind are made by Stata alone, with its own in-house developers then working to polish the selected user-contributed applications and integrate them seamlessly into the standard software package. As a rule, users make their own developments available at no cost to Stata – the incentive being instead the additional creation of value on the part of the company. After all, the motivation for working on the contribution in the first place was the use of this self-developed application within the individual's own scientific work.

We would also like to look at one last example, which shows how users have employed full-scale commons-based peer production to utterly transform what was once an industry organized along traditional lines (our discussion here is based on that of von Hippel 2005). Kitesurfing is currently one of the hottest up-and-coming sports. It originated within the surfing community, with surfers wanting to achieve greater height and distance when making jumps. Initial trials were made using a surfboard combined with a sail from hang-gliding equipment. Beginning with these initial prototypes, the sport has since developed into a sizeable niche industry with many devoted followers. This kitesurfing industry is an example of a situation where customers act as product developers to change the parameters of the industrial value creation process. These customers not only play a decisive role in equipment development, but have now moved to occupy many other positions in the industry that were earlier the responsibility of professional manufacturers – most especially the coordination of the production process.

The manufacturing companies, often founded by kitesurfers who have made their hobby their career, today form part of an industry worth some US$ 100 million, chiefly responsible for kite development, production, and distribution. A broad spectrum of skills is required for the successful realization of a new kite product, including knowledge of materials and material characteristics (sail), expertise in aerodynamics and physics (sail form), and know-how in mechanical engineering (roping systems). In developing new designs, manufacturers are limited in general to the knowledge that they have themselves gained during in-house research and development work, with such R&D units generally employing no more than three to five members of staff. The end results therefore tend to be enhancements and improvements for existing designs rather than any radical new developments.

The customers, however, command a far greater potential and are not tied to any particular company. Set up and managed by a number of dedicated kitesurfers, a whole range of Internet communities is in existence today, whose members busy themselves with developing, publishing, and discussing potential kite designs. At zeroprestige.org[15], for example, users can utilize open source design software (similar to a CAD package) to develop new kite designs and subsequently upload them for other users to access. Other users can then utilize these designs as the starting point for their own developments. They may of course discover a radical new approach to kite design in the process. Among the many hundreds of participating users, a number of people actually work with new materials in their day job. Others are perhaps physics students or work as wind tunnel technicians at an automobile manufacturer. It is often the case that the group of customer developers has access to a far larger pool of talent and skills than that which is typical for a single manufacturer. The result is thus a multitude of new developments, tests, modifications, and, ultimately, new designs for kites, all of which are provided freely to all members of the community (under an open source license).

Kitesurfing is a particularly compelling example, since, as users, the customers go a step further: after all, what use is the most innovative design for a new kite, if it only exists in a file stored on a computer? Enterprising customers have discovered that every major lake has its own sailmaker-in-residence, who can work with CAD file formats. Accordingly, customers can download their chosen design, take the file to the sailmaker and ask for it to be turned into a professional end product. Since this process involves zero innovation risk and development costs for the manufacturer, kites produced in this fashion are often up to 50% cheaper than products manufactured by professional kite makers – and often deliver a superior performance. Within this system, the users also take on the work of coordinating the manufacturing process. Should this system become more widespread, it is easy to imagine how customers may come to "annex" certain parts of the industry or force providers into assuming the role of mere "manufacturers." And all the while, these users are driven not by the desire to increase profits or market share, but by the hope of attaining the best possible product for their own use. The users that participate in this process have understood that their common goal can be best achieved by an innovation process that is not closed, but open – and one that furthermore distributes its end products freely to all of the members of the system. The participation of the individual invokes reactions and contributions from other users, thereby contributing to increased value for all.

Competence in interaction as the central challenge within interactive value creation

The successful implementation of interactive value creation requires competence in interaction from companies and customers alike. On the company side, this requirement is realized within systems for organization, leadership, and motivation that foster interaction, as well as structures and tools supporting information and communication (e.g., toolkits, interaction platforms). Assessed in terms of the resource-based view, competence in interaction is elevated to a core competence of the organization (Pralahad/Hamel 1990). This theory not only views the presence of resources as important, but also the various ways in which different resources can be interconnected with one another. Core competences themselves depend less on traditional production factors such as engineering or capital resources, requiring instead "organizational resources" in the sense of standard procedures, routines, and methods of coordination and management.

If innovation is generated primarily within networks populated by a variety of organizational types, then the workflow process that governs the manufacture of the good needs to be extended beyond the internal manufacturing organization. Central to this activity is the definition of the means by which a number of different agents and their contributions (offered for a variety of different reasons) will be integrated into a networked innovation and value creation process. Here, incentive structures fostering interaction have an important role to play. Suitable company-internal incentives must exist that reward both the transfer of customer know-how into the company and the uptake of external knowledge. It is appreciated that not all companies have policies concerning user input that are quite so receptive as those of Stata or Threadless. Indeed, for many manufacturers it is an entirely novel idea to think that users can make a (superior) contribution to the development of their own products. Often, it is a few forward-thinking units within a company who take the initiative of launching a project for integrating customer knowledge and start encouraging user contributions. These contributions must, however, be processed and utilized by other departments within the company. This transfer process has been the subject of a discussion within innovation management that identifies a problem it terms "not invented here syndrome" (NIH syndrome). Katz and Allen (1982) define the NIH syndrome as follows: "The tendency of a project group of stable composition to believe that it possesses a monopoly of knowledge in its field, which leads it to reject new ideas from outsiders to the detriment of its performance." Classic cases of the NIH phenomenon in action have been identified in different departments within the same company (e.g., the resistance of the software engineers to incorporating input provided by the marketing department). One may assume that resistance to external knowledge will be many dimensions greater than that shown to input from company colleagues. Within the context of interactive value creation between customers and a manufacturing company, this means that knowledge provided by external sources can expect to meet resistance from at least some of the internal users of this know-how.

A classic approach to solving the problem of NIH syndrome promotes the use of "gatekeepers" (Allen 1977) – individuals that connect the development team with external knowledge sources and who also act to filter out irrelevant information. Gatekeepers possess both mechanisms and incentives to share their knowledge of external knowledge with appropriate portions of the wider organization (see Allen 1977 and Gemünden 1981; Moenaert/Souder 1990 on the design of the gatekeeper role). Accordingly, companies are advised to set up gatekeepers who are given the specialized role of accepting customer information and feeding it into the internal company development processes. Microsoft provides us with an example of this strategy (Prahalad/Ramaswamy 2000). Microsoft maintains a group of about 1,500 key users with leadership characteristics (webmasters, programmers, or software distributors) – its "Microsoft Buddies" – who deliver valuable input for the long-term development of Microsoft software.[16] Members of this group are included as primary beta testers for new releases, offer detailed feedback about existing products on the market, and supply ideas for new kinds of functionality. In return, they receive free software packages and are invited to attend special events. To reduce the occurrence of NIH syndrome between the ideas of the "Buddies" and the company itself, Microsoft has appointed "Liaison Officers" – gatekeepers stationed between Microsoft's internal developer teams and the external users. Liaison Officers, managers with years of experience at Microsoft, maintain a large internal network while also possessing a certain hierarchical clout – making them ideal candidates for driving the integration of user input.

Another strategy for establishing competence in interaction at the incentives level is to create an open corporate structure. Work in this field emphasizes three aspects: the leveraging of internal knowledge management (since this is faced with the exact same challenges in the distribution and utilization of local knowledge within different domains), the advantages gained by decentralized company structures, and the delegation of decision-making onto the operative level (Foss/Laursen/Pedersen 2005). The idea is to shift decision-making responsibility down to a level where the relevant knowledge for both discussing and executing the decision is to be found. The rationale is that information transfer within a company is often characterized by "sticky information," which complicates the movement of knowledge from one location to another. To what degree this reintegration of planning and administrative tasks is completed is largely dependent on the granularity of the approach and the objectives at hand. The principle of subsidiarity is nonetheless generally adopted as a guideline for the decentralization of functions (Picot/Reichwald/Wigand 2003): responsibility for decision-making and results should be kept as low in the hierarchy as possible – i.e., sited as near as possible to the actual process of value creation. Accordingly, low-level decision-making responsibilities enable the company to achieve far greater flexibility, with their many decentralized and customer-oriented feedback loops and the absence of long, error-prone decision-making processes. At the same time, employee motivation must be strengthened via a holistic attitude to task completion, plus incentives for behavior that is congruent with the market.

Close cooperation with external parties that includes the transference of knowledge may, however, lead some employees to fear that they are thereby making themselves expendable and thus, in the worst scenario, endangering their very position in the company. Equally, at a company level, cooperation on innovation often leads to anxiety about the business impairing its ability to compete. It is therefore necessary to introduce clear and comprehensible measures for generating trust in these areas and to use targeted "trust management" to establish a foundation for successful cooperation. However, much depends on the operational and supra-operational systems for organization, leadership, and incentives in place: these will influence the design of processes that can lead to successful innovation networks directly, while also determining which factors are capable of promoting or stifling such activities within the various departments.

Opportunities and limitations posed by interactive value creation

As we have already seen, there are also appreciable limits on interactive value creation. We will include a brief discussion of a few of these here (for a detailed appraisal see Reichwald/Piller 2006). These limitations indicate that the traditional models of organizing the division of work for value creation will continue to maintain their validity, for not all tasks that require completion within an economy can be resolved using the model of interactive value creation. Some fundamental limitations of the model can be found in the trade-off between the granularity of task subdivision and transaction costs, as well as in the level at which participant motivation can be maintained.

Concerning the trade-off between the granularity of task subdivision and transaction costs, one may state that the more suitable a value creation task is for subdivision into many pieces (i.e., the greater its granularity factor), the easier it will be for a greater percentage of the task to be handed off to a network consisting of customers and users. This fact will also make it easier to utilize specialization effects within such a network. However, these individual contributions to value creation will need to be coordinated and integrated within the company: where task subdivision is highly granular, high internal costs will be incurred. Accordingly, for tasks that cannot be represented easily at a digital level, utilizing interactive value creation will prove far harder than it is for wholly digital goods.

And yet it is surprisingly easy today to separate the informational part and the physical component in many areas: t-shirts, a classic example of a physical product, have been transformed by Threadless into an informational good that leaves the digital realm only shortly before production. The same is true of the kite sails in our kitesurfing example. The OSCAR project, on the other hand – an ambitious initiative to build an "open-source car" – has so far proved to be an almost complete failure. One of the problems here seems to be the difficulty in coordinating a complex technical procedure such as the development of an automobile using only a decentralized network as the medium.

Participant motivation: a further limit is imposed by participant motivation. Up until now, the enthusiasm of users and companies has seemed to be truly boundless. Expertise supplied by customers or users is simply viewed as a vast untapped pool of knowledge that is there to be exploited. Many companies are now trying to utilize the skills of their customers and users – with some showing remarkable ineptitude. (Piller (2006) discusses an initiative from the Kraft organization as an example of how not to go about this.) However, if such initiatives are not connected to a clear system of incentives, then the user's initial feelings of euphoria ("The company is at last listening to what I say!") will rapidly modulate into disillusionment ("They're just stealing my ideas!"), and the user will no longer be prepared to participate.

An important concept that needs reiterating at this juncture is that of the free and non-proprietary availability of resultant knowledge. This is not only productive – as has been discussed above – but also has the power to motivate (fairness – above all, the immediate right of use for the people contributing the knowledge). Yet a great many of the major business models employed in contemporary companies restrict this kind of openness. Accordingly, companies must be extremely well-informed about the reasons for customer participation and offer incentives that target this motivation (see also Brockhoff 2005). Many companies, however, lack not only knowledge in this area but also fail to even grasp the principles.

Interactive value creation cannot therefore be seen merely as a way to "outsource" internal tasks to the company periphery. On the contrary, it demands the active participation of the supplier, who must also possess certain resources and competences. Real-world proof of this competence in interaction is offered by systems for organization, leadership, and incentives and also by systems and tools that support information and communication – ensuring the efficiency, effectiveness, and usability of the interaction workflow. It is our opinion that few companies have so far established this kind of proof of their competence in interaction.

Accordingly, interactive value creation is not an all-conquering system that will drive out old value creation systems overnight. Many companies are only just beginning to implement interactive value creation processes. One should recall that even the traditional mass production methods required many decades before they reached their present level of perfection in modern manufacturing systems. It will therefore take an appreciable amount of time before interactive value creation becomes a widespread phenomenon. There is, however, a new factor at work: unlike the traditional company structures, subject to the inertia of company management, today's environment sees employees and customers as factors for change, working to make a difference together. Yet interactive value creation is not universally applicable. It should instead be seen as a complement to the tried-and-tested methods and instruments used in the management of innovation and value creation. While the old principles will retain their validity, the new methods will establish the foundation for increased competitive advantage.

WORKS CITED

Allen, Thomas (1977). Managing the flow of technology. Cambridge, MA: MIT Press.

Becker, Gary S. (1965). A theory of the allocation of time. In: Economic Journal, 75: 493-517.

Benkler, Yochai (2002). Coase's Penguin, or: Linux and the nature of the firm. The Yale Law Journal, 112: 369-446 [www.benkler.org/CoasesPenguin.html]

Benkler, Yochai (2006). The wealth of networks. New Haven: Yale University Press.

Brockhoff, Klaus (2005). Konflikte bei der Einbeziehung von Kunden in die Produktentwicklung. In: Zeitschrift für Betriebswirtschaft, 75:9, 859-877.

Deci, Edward L.; Koestner, Richard; Ryan, Richard M. (1999). Meta-analytic review of experiments: Examining the effects of extrinsic rewards on intrinsic motivation. In: Psychological Bulletin 125:3, 627-668.

Foss, Nicolai J.; Laursen, Karl; Perdersen, Torben (2005). Organizing to gain from user interaction: The role of organizational practices for absorptive and innovative capacities. Working paper, Copenhagen Business School, Center for Strategic Management and Globalization, Copenhagen.

Gemünden, Hans Georg (1981). Innovationsmarketing. Tübingen: Mohr.

Gibbert, Michael; Leibold, Marius; Probst, Gilbert (2002). Five styles of customer knowledge management, and how smart companies use them to create value. European Management Journal, 20:5, 459-469.

Gutenberg, Erich (1951). Grundlagen der Betriebswirtschaftslehre. Volume 1: Die Produktion. Berlin/Heidelberg: Springer.

Hammer, Michael; Champy, James (1993). Reengineering the corporation. New York: Harper Business.

Huff, Anne S.; Piller, Frank; Möslein, Kathrin; Fredberg, Tobias (2006): Creating centripetal innovation capacity, Proceedings of the AOM 2006 Meeting, Atlanta.

Katz, Ralph; Allen, Thomas (1982). Investigating the Not Invented Here (NIH) syndrome: A look at the performance, tenure, and communication patterns of 50 R&D projects. In: R&D Management, 12: 7-19.

Kosiol, Erich (1959). Grundlagen und Methoden der Organisationsforschung. Berlin: Springer.

Lakhani, Karim (2005). The core and the periphery in self-organizing and distributed innovation systems. Ph.D. thesis, MIT Sloan School of Management, Cambridge, MA.

Lakhani, Karim R.; von Hippel, Eric (2002). How Open Source Software Works: "Free" User-to-User Assistance. Research Policy, 32:6, 923-943.

Lancaster, Kelvin J. (1966). A new approach to consumer theory. In: Journal of Political Economy, 74: 132-157.

Moenaert, Rudy K.; Souder, William E. (1990). An information transfer model for integrating marketing and R&D personnel in new product development projects. In: Journal of Product Innovation Management, 7:1, 91-107.

Möslein, Kathrin (2005). Der Markt für Managementwissen. Wiesbaden: Gabler.

Ogawa, Susumu; Piller, Frank T. (2006). Reducing the risk of new product development. In: MIT Sloan Management Review, 48:1, 65-72.

Picot, Arnold; Reichwald, Ralf (1994). Auflösung der Unternehmung? Vom Einfluss der IuK-Technik auf Organisationsstrukturen und Kooperationsformen. Zeitschrift für Betriebswirtschaft, 64:5, 547-570.

Picot, Arnold; Reichwald, Ralf; Wigand, Rolf (2003). Die grenzenlose Unternehmung. 5th edition, Wiesbaden: Gabler.

Piller, Frank (2006): Kraft Foods Crowdsources Innovation Process to Customers; Blog posting to "Mass Customization & Open Innovation News," [tinyurl.com/j9pwm] on June 3.

Porter, Michael (1985). Competitive advantage: creating and sustaining superior performance. New York: The Free Press.

Porter, Michael (1996). What is strategy? In: Harvard Business Review, 74:6, 61-78.

Prahalad, Coimbatore (CK); Hamel, Gary (1990). The core competencies of the corporation. Harvard Business Review, 68:3, 79-91.

Prahalad, Coimbatore (CK); Ramaswamy, Venkatram (2000). Co-opting customer competence. In: Harvard Business Review, 79:1, 79-87.

Ramirez, Rafael (1999). Value co-production: intellectual origins and Implications for practice and research. Strategic Management Journal, 20:1, 49-65.

Reichwald, Ralf; Piller, Frank (2006). Interaktive Wertschöpfung: Open Innovation, Individualisierung und neue Formen der Arbeitsteilung. Wiesbaden: Gabler [Download at www.open-innovation.de].

von Hippel, Eric (2005). Democratizing innovation. Cambridge, MA: MIT Press.

Don Tapscott
Winning with the Enterprise 2.0

Today we're at a defining moment in business history – the threshold of a dramatic shift in the way that firms are organized, innovate, and create value. Information technology and new networked business structures are removing the sources of friction in our economy, producing major dimensions of change that every firm must address. A new breed of open, networked organization – the Enterprise 2.0 – is emerging. Evidence is mounting that companies that shift along the dimensions of the new model perform and compete better.

Due to profound changes in the global business environment, information technology, and management thinking and experience, a fundamental change is occurring in how companies compete. In particular, the rise of pervasive, networked IT is enabling new business strategies and designs – that enable firms to create differentiated value and/or lower cost structures – and therefore competitive advantage. A new approach to business is required. It is a new model of the firm, or the Enterprise 2.0 as I and others have described it. Others may know it better as the Open, Networked Enterprise (ONE), a label we've also used to illustrate the shift. Such enterprises orchestrate resources, create value, and compete very differently than traditional firms. They also drive important changes in their respective industries and even the rules of competition. Research and experience show that those who understand these changes can gain rapid advantage in their markets and build sustainable businesses.

This article lays out a description of the Enterprise 2.0 and evidence for dimensions of change. And if there is one theme that cuts across all and defines the new enterprise, it is collaboration.

The age of collaboration

Collaboration is the new foundation of competitiveness. Normally the term collaboration conjures up images of office workers interacting effectively together. True, knowledge is the ability to take effective action. The exchange of knowledge among people allows them to communicate complex ideas and to collaborate in creating value.

But the concept is changing. By "collaboration" we mean the increasing richness of means by which objects (things, people, and firms) can work together enhanced by the medium of the Internet. We have described this as the fundamental transition of the Internet from being a communications platform to a computation platform. We have investigated five cascading levels of collaboration sought by leading firms today (See Figure 1.) The lower levels cascade up to the higher levels which in turn inform and set the context for lower levels.

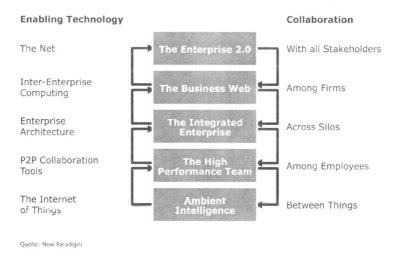

Figure 1: Cascading collaboration for competitive advantage

Level 1: Collaboration among things

Billions, soon trillions of physical objects are becoming smart, imbued with knowledge and connected by an Internet of Things. Pervasive computing is giving rise to ambient intelligence as we become increasingly surrounded by things that can sense and collaborate. Our research investigated three aspects: the shifting "object of interest," granularity, and scale (Drucker 1988; Drucker 1989).

Object of interest

At every major stage in the evolution of IT, there has been a distinct technology and associated "object of interest," such as the mainframe computer and the firm; the PC and the desktop; and the handheld computer (in all its guises) and the individual. The primary object of interest dictates where the bulk of innovation and technological advance is found (e.g., game consoles drive graphics technology, MP3 players and cameras drive memory, handhelds drive miniaturization). Each shift in the object of interest has been a discontinuity.

Today we are heading rapidly into the next stage where the object of interest is the "thing" – a car, a soup can, a meadow. Associating an intelligent, communicating device, such as an RFID tag, with a "thing" brings it into the ambit of corporate networks, the Internet, or even a self-organizing ad hoc network of other things (e.g., home entertainment devices). The shift in the object of interest opens new opportunities. When the object is a person and the computing device is "cell phone like," the opportunity is to create or exploit a new channel of interaction. When the object is a thing, the opportunity is to increase the level of control or awareness of physical processes (e.g. logistics, telematics).

Granularity

As the Internet penetrates every nook and cranny of the physical world, it connects a myriad of ever-smaller objects. Granularity is the increasingly finer breakdown of knowledge about what is happening in the world – for example, knowing where things are at the item level rather than the truck level, knowing about events as they happen rather than some time later, and knowing the state of the world at a micro level, such as the paths of shoppers through the store rather than just what they bought. This has important implications for precisely how a firm can manage its operations, and it raises the bar for what it means to be agile and responsive. It also increases the complexity of the problem you must solve when you try to manage a system optimally.

Every industry will incorporate the effects of granularity differently. For example, one that is heavily involved in the movement of physical goods (e.g., discrete manufacturing, retail, healthcare) will be dramatically affected by the inclusion of these goods in the Internet (through RFID tags, wireless MEMS, etc.). Meanwhile a bit-based industry like broadcasting will find its opportunities in the evolution of personal devices.

Scale

Ambient intelligence enables firms to scale – and think about scale – in radical new ways. A world of interconnected, intelligent objects – sensing/responding to ever more granular events enables firms to compete through scale in ways previously unimagined. To some extent, the ability of a firm to collect enormous amounts of data about its operations and transactions will be matched by advances in communications technology (e.g., self-organizing mesh networks), processor power (e.g., Blue Gene), storage technologies, and analytic software (such as business intelligence systems). For example, storage is now nearly free, so data can be stored at a highly disaggregated level, and reduced to information as required, via OLAP / business intelligence systems. Firms need to foresee and play emerging wild cards. As computers spread into the world of things, they become unimaginably abundant. As a result, we will need to design machines that can thrive "in the wild," forming relationships with other machines on the fly to accomplish goals that we cannot fully predict. We see this already in the formation of ad hoc wireless mesh networks, where nodes sense the presence of one another and form robust, self-healing networks through relatively simple message exchange. This trend will only accelerate. The home is an obvious environment where one would want, say, entertainment devices to interoperate without external configuration, wiring, and the like.

Level 2: Collaboration among employees

For two decades, companies have worked to harness the power of teams. As Peter Drucker said in 1988, "Traditional departments will serve as guardians of standards, as centers for training and the assignment of specialists; they won't be where the work gets done. That will happen largely in task-focused teams." It has long been understood that business teams can deliver faster responses to changes in the business environment and increasing customer demands. Teams can help bring together the right people at the right time, from many disciplines and parts of the formal structure, to battle competition at home and abroad. Business teams can help organizations dramatically improve their cost structures through the elimination of traditional bureaucracies or by avoiding the creation of new ones. Genuine collaboration happens as much around the water cooler as it does in the boardroom. In the same way that architects design shared interactive community spaces, digital environments also need to offer collaborative content opportunities – both formal and informal.

On one end of the spectrum, firms can encourage fluid impromptu interactions (via a "digital water cooler"). On the other, firms can think about how content collaboration should be built directly into everyday work and business processes. Building new thinking on knowledge management right into the structure of work is much more effective than treating knowledge management as an isolated activity – one which competes with people's time and other priorities. It should augment work, not detract from it. As ever more work and interactions occur in digital spaces, the ability to build knowledge management into every-day tasks increases.

Today, a wide range of new tools and disciplines are appearing on the scene, enabling team collaboration for virtually all knowledge work, with goals such as innovation, agility, and competitiveness. In the IT&CA project of Collaborative Knowledge and Competitive Advantage, Hubert Saint-Onge discusses the use of peer-to-peer (P2P) technology within organizations. Maturing quickly in the last three years, it has allowed employees to operate in a decentralized manner to fulfill individual and common goals. Peers share capabilities to provide data and/or services, and can make or break partnerships at will. Open source software supporting P2P interactions has made this option widely available. P2P networks can give individuals access to group documents anywhere, at any time. They can also help develop connections with customers and suppliers. IBM, for example, offers a free internal service that allows any employee to start a blog, resulting in over 1,000 active blogs. The BBC claims 600 active internal bloggers. These technologies have already demonstrated the ability to transform organizations and industries. However, the trend is still new and it is difficult to say where it will lead. Although organizational use is relatively marginal at this point, there is little doubt these tools will soon be added to the growing arsenal of collaborative technology.

Level 3: Collaboration across silos

IT-enabled processes extend beyond the business team to the enterprise. Like teams, the concept of enterprise integration has been around for some time. As I wrote in „The Digital Economy" over a decade ago (Tapscott 1996), business process reengineering was useful because it highlighted the importance of designing business processes which are horizontal, that is, they cut across old organizational boundaries. Customers in the information age have become better informed and more demanding. They often require fully integrated solutions, customized to their ever-changing tastes. The organizational challenge of delivering such products, services, and increasingly, experiences has forced companies to redesign their business models. New models must transcend traditional business segments in order to build the capability to deliver integrated value offerings.

Further, most large organizations today are geographically dispersed. This fuels a need for people to communicate and work together while being separated by great distances. Networking technologies allow companies to run cohesive yet decentralized operations by linking employees in virtual teams and communities of practice. However, in practice, most new processes are fairly low level; they are restricted to one department or perhaps span two or three departments. Because of the rise of standards and the feasibility of implementing a service-oriented, enterprise technology architecture, it is possible to think bigger – to create entire businesses that are "integrated."

Still, today's typical enterprise is locked into technologies of the past – islands of technology that codify old business practices and old organizational structures. In the twentieth century, firms implemented computer systems when the technologies matured to the point where cost beneficial applications were feasible. Such systems tended to be planned within the context of traditional structures – discrete systems for production, marketing, financial management, and research. Technology was not used to change the nature of work but to automate old ways of working – in other words, paving the cow paths. As a result, companies remain saddled with legacy systems which are impediments, rather than catalysts, to change.

This problem is non-trivial. Many legacy islands are old enough to vote. They are not simply "code museums" as some pundits have said. They are operational systems upon which businesses depend – so rolling a bulldozer into the data center is not a feasible fix. Worse, because they lack vision for enterprise systems, firms often perpetuate the legacy with each new investment. Every dollar spent makes the islands bigger, rather than better, for the future. Companies need to create the conditions that mean new investments contribute to a desired future rather than perpetuating the past.

Today the Net, the rise of Web services, and service-oriented architectures open vast opportunities to reduce coordinating costs within the firm – in turn leading to deep changes in the structures of enterprises.

The new approach to architecture is based on principles defined by business people, not technologists. A holistic approach presents the enterprise through business, operational, systems, and technology views. It is based on an abstract model of business activities, one that does not depend on the changing contingencies of processes and organizational structure. It can be described as a service-oriented reference model of operational capabilities.

Such enterprise integration provides the backbone for the new enterprise. It enables an organization to move beyond the old hierarchy because layers of management are not required when information is instantly available electronically. It enables the enterprise to function as a cohesive unit by providing corporate-wide information for decision-making and new competitive enterprise applications that transcend autonomous business units or teams.

At the same time, such architectures provide a platform for collaboration within business teams – while maintaining an enterprise capability. Business units can become viewed as networked service functions, working in a modular, flexible organizational structure.

Level 4: Collaboration among firms

Central to the IT&CA point of view is the idea that collaboration is changing the design of businesses – and the axis of collaboration operates among firms, not just inside them. Vertically integrated firms are giving way to focused companies that collaborate with others in business webs (b-webs).

Collaboration costs between firms historically caused companies to vertically integrate rather than partner. Today, the Internet has dramatically reduced the cost of coordinating work among firms. This is leading to the biggest change in the architecture of the corporation in a century – firms are un-bundling (disaggregating), with the resulting components re-aggregated into new economic players depending on the effects of scale and scope economies. This creates a fluid environment in which the boundaries of the firm can (and do) move – creating new opportunities for value creation, value migration, and strategic cost control. The tonic of the market is being brought to bear on every function in the firm.

While rich collaboration methods improve the ability of the firm to lower costs, it is innovation, agility, speed, and other value-related objectives that are energizing this change in corporate architecture.

The reason is that new markets can evolve in unexpected directions, demanding capabilities that the firm does not possess. It is frequently possible to assemble best-of-breed capabilities from a set of firms into a winning production-distribution system, and to do this rapidly. The inherent agility of a b-web therefore provides competitive benefits, at least in the short run, and will dominate other organizational forms that do not have modularity built in. Most companies today are moving in this direction. Focusing on b-webs is a necessary but insufficient condition for competitiveness. Firms need to make the right choices regarding boundaries – what is in and what is out – a key theme of this research. They need to design the optimal b-web type – agoras (eBay), aggregations (Tesco), value chains (Foxconn), self-organizing alliances (Linux), and distributive networks (iTunes). They also need to design the optimal b-web mix of types as any company should usually orchestrate resources through some combination of these. They also need to build high-performance b-webs – taking steps to ensure that partner relationships are designed and managed effectively, that goals are aligned, that transparency is harnessed to improve b-web metabolism, and so on.

Competitiveness remains central to profitability, growth, and business success. It is true that in many emerging markets competitors do not exist. Disruptive innovations enable firms to create entirely new markets. Yet in the long run, firms still need to compete – fundamentally through differentiated value or lower cost structures. If collaboration is central to competitiveness, rather than talking about "collaborative advantage," it makes sense to discuss the "collaborative edge." Collaboration also demands a better appreciation of the role of business context in strategy. That is because you need to think of strategy as a system in which the outcomes depend not only on your actions, but on the actions of competitors as well – it is a dynamic system with non-linear outcomes. You must engage in systems that you do not fully control. The evidence is strong that a myriad of quantitative changes are becoming qualitative – and that the nature of the corporation and the dynamics of competitiveness are changing. We call the new model the Enterprise 2.0.

The Enterprise 2.0

Networking enables collaboration – as explained above on four levels. But collaboration demands something relatively new in business – openness. If you consider the vernacular, "open" is a loaded term – rich with meaning.

Being Open		
Characteristic		**Vernacular Expression**
Possibilities	→	"open for business"
Candor, Transparency	→	"open book"
Standards	→	"open systems"
Networking	→	"open door policy"
Innovation	→	"finding and opening"
Listening	→	"open ears"
Engagement	→	"open arms"
Flexibility and agility	→	"open to suggestion"
Sharing	→	"open source"
Access	→	"open bar"
Freedom	→	"open society"
Expansiveness	→	"open range", "opening up"
Replenishment	→	"open stock"
Complexity	→	"open ended"
Sincerity	→	"open hearted"
Beginnings	→	"opener"
Lack of Restrictions	→	"open season", "open shop", "open market", "open skies"

Quelle: New Paradigm

Figure 2: Being open

Modus operandi

From hierarchical to self-organizing

Self-organization is often depicted as a fringe phenomenon – the likes of MP3 and the hacker quasi-anarchists who built Linux and Firefox. While it is true that much innovation begins at the fringes, David Ticoll and Phil Hood (2005) of the IT&CA project explain that increasingly, large Lighthouse firms are turning to self-organization models in order to reduce costs, speed time to market, neutralize competitors, and capture customers and engage their loyalty. In each of these companies, the business case for engaging and collaborating with self-organized communities is measured in dollars to the top and bottom line. Companies such as IBM (software), Eli Lilly (pharmaceuticals), Harley-Davidson (manufacturing), eBay (retail), Procter & Gamble (consumer goods and health), and dozens more are discovering how to make self-organization a key component of the modern day strategic arsenal.

Self-organization succeeds because it leverages a style of peer production that works more effectively than hierarchical management or open markets for certain tasks. Its greatest impact is in the production of information goods, and its initial effects are generally most visible in the production of software, media, entertainment, and culture.

Our basic assumption is that self-organization is here to stay. Technology has permanently lowered the cost barriers for self-organizing networks to operate and changed the economic tradeoffs that individuals make to join them. Self-organized networks increasingly create more value than firms or markets. As self-organization becomes accepted as a viable method of production, more processes within the organization will move from being hierarchically directed, proprietary, and closed to self-organizing, shared, and open.

Not all examples of self-organization are benign or exploitable. Within a single industry, the development of opportunities for self-organized or open-source collaboration can be beneficial, neutral, or highly competitive to individual firms or some combination of at least two of these. Consider publishing media. Blogs, wikis, chat rooms, search, advertising auctions, peer-to-peer downloading, and personal broadcasting, to name but a few, represent new ways to communicate and transact. In each of these, the traditionally passive buyers of editorial and advertising take active, participatory roles in value co-creation. Some of these examples pose dire threats to existing business models – others will have mostly positive effects on future value creation.

Our research on this topic helps firms model the self-organization challenge, gives them a language to describe the terrain, and a roadmap for leveraging this new model. The focus is on how organizations can successfully engage and collaborate with self-organized communities inside and outside the firm to achieve competitive advantage. Key questions that any business planner should want to answer with regard to self-organization are:

- How do self-organizing systems operate to create value in business, and how can firms engage and collaborate most effectively with them?

- What are the conditions that enable self-organization to develop in a particular field?

- How do I respond to threats and opportunities created via self-organization?

The increasingly interlinked web of networks and intelligent devices has become a key driver of self-organizing activity in business, politics, and society. Without these networks, there is no Linux, no Napster or BitTorrent, no Moveon.org, no multiplayer gaming. Firms increasingly find themselves interacting with self-organizing phenomena, from open source development communities in software to open research markets in biology to underground peer-to-peer networks in entertainment. The poster child example of self-organization is widespread, distributed software development. However, the opportunity to leverage or piggyback on self-organizing group behavior for competitive advantage is increasingly available in every industry and every sphere of activity.

From plan and push to engage and tailor

As firms open up and become networked, a new modus operandi is emerging – affecting the way they bring products to market and treat customers.

A little history. Ticoll and Hood (2005) explain that before the rise of the modern enterprise and, in particular, the limited liability corporation, economic activity was mostly small scale. Farmers and craftspeople sold their goods in markets, where local conditions of supply and demand applied. There was very little production planning, forecasting, or marketing. If you wanted a coat, you engaged the seamstress to make one. If you wanted eggs, you bought them in the market or haggled with a local farmer.

Beginning in the nineteenth century, the rise of railroads and other large firms changed the economic production model. Large firms centralized resources and decision-making and captured huge supply-side economies of scale. Centralized planning and marketing replaced the volatility of uncontrolled markets.

This mode of operation, sometimes called plan and push, was extraordinarily well adapted to the post-war years in North America. Production barriers in many fields led to oligopolies. Large manufacturers operated with fewer competitive threats and more opportunity to direct marketplace activities.

Companies were organized vertically, with tight control over proprietary resources and knowledge. In the plan and push era, firms competed by way of superior internal capabilities. The sense and respond model loosened the firm – supply chains became more extended, standards more open, and hierarchy was flattened as work transitioned toward services and individual knowledge products. Competition shifted to competition between supply chains, not just firms.

Today, the pace of change and the dynamic demands of customers are such that firms can no longer depend on internal capabilities to meet external needs. Nor can they depend on tightly coupled relationships with several b-web partners to keep up with customer desires for speed, innovation, and control. Instead, firms must engage and collaborate in a dynamic fashion with everyone – partners, competitors, educational and government institutions, and most of all customers. This is depicted in Figure 3:

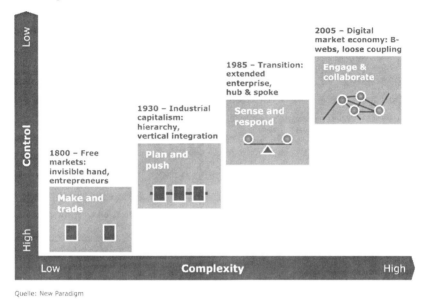

Quelle: New Paradigm

Figure 3: The rise of engage and collaborate

Designing for self-organization and engagement

Many successful self-organizing systems are deliberately architected – from eBay's auction system to Overture's advertiser network (now part of Yahoo!). However, that is not to say that leveraging self-organizing networks is easy, something even the strongest proponents of self-organizing systems admit.

Architecting self-organizing systems is a complex task requiring a deep knowledge of stakeholder interests. It also requires an understanding of the complex connection between the rules that govern the system and the macro behaviors likely to emerge from that system as a result – a process that is half art and half science.

Second Life vice president Cory Ondrejka describes many design challenges in constructing the building blocks of self-organizing networks, which he calls "atomistic construction." Atomistic construction is "not widely used because it is extremely difficult to implement." The challenge is building a foundation that is predictable enough to use on one hand, yet diverse enough to produce emergent behaviors that "interact in interesting and unexpected ways to allow experimenters and innovators to create truly new creations."

The challenges of designing Second Life's self-organizing virtual environment are not unique. Similar design issues are raised in other self-organizing environments as well, whether it is the subtleties inherent in ratings systems like those offered by eBay, Slashdot, and Amazon, or the challenges in architecting electronic marketplaces. In securities markets for instance, it is the market microstructures that matter (tick size, identity, order book displays, and order priority). According to Plexus Group, microstructures and execution algorithms are extremely important. "The issue is crucial because in an era of electronic trading, it's the execution algorithm that determines trade flow with huge consequences."

Designs of such systems cannot be arbitrarily determined, but must reflect information about stakeholders, their relationships, and power structures. Trust and legitimacy are another essential ingredient of self-organizing systems. While healthy self-organizing systems are extremely robust and fault-tolerant, underlying that strength is a faith in the overall system in which they participate. When the legitimacy of trust of the system is called into question, the strength of the system can evaporate just as quickly, according to Charles Smith, "this is not a case where trial and error works very well, because if you blow it and something goes wrong and you lose your trust in the marketplace in these areas, you may never recover. This is one of the places where if you make a mistake up front you may be gone."[17]

Leveraging self-organizing systems also requires what may be a significant shift in culture for some firms – letting go of control. The very qualities that make self-organizing systems so valuable – management of complexity, flexibility, fault-tolerance, innovation, customer contributions, and efficient resource allocation – require a unique maintenance philosophy. There are no control levers or chains of command. Rather, there are community engagement, feedback mechanisms, and system design characteristics. More complicated still is that while on-going participant feedback is an essential ingredient in maintaining (note: not "managing") self-organizing systems, many participants will fail to appreciate all system design considerations – sometimes asking for features detrimental to the ultimate health of the system. Complex give and take, knowledge of system design, and attention to relationships and information flows help maintain the health and growth of self-organizing systems.

To acquire the capabilities needed to compete, organizations must be open with knowledge – exchanging it, as appropriate, with customers, suppliers and partners. For meaningful change that builds and sustains competitive advantage, organizations must create vibrant knowledge networks that individuals feel compelled to join. When individuals or firms attempt to operate in a closed system, they eliminate sources of renewal and ultimately jeopardize their survival in the marketplace.

Emerging technologies provide increasingly effective virtual spaces for collaboration – where individuals purposefully exchange knowledge and capture it to benefit others inside and outside the enterprise. Effective collaboration and the capture of content it engenders lead to capability development.

Therefore, organizations must deploy technology platforms for (a) the exchange of knowledge and (b) the generation of and access to content. We refer to this as a content/collaboration platform. Powerful content/collaboration tools are already entering organizations, and not necessarily through top-down enterprise procurement, but through bottom-up acquisition by the individuals who most need them. E-mail, instant messaging, blogs, wikis, and mobile phones are just a few examples of the simple technologies aiding networked collaboration and knowledge management at the individual level. While most of these technologies (with the exception of mobile phones) originated outside corporate walls, they are gaining popularity within firms, sometimes despite policies to the contrary.

Transparency and competitive advantage

As David Ticoll and I explain in our book „The Naked Corporation: How the Age of Transparency Will Revolutionize Business," there is a powerful rising force in business, one that has far-reaching implications for most everyone (Tapscott/Ticoll 2005). Nascent for half a century, this force has quietly gained momentum through the last decade; it is now triggering profound changes across the corporate world. The force is transparency. This is far more than the obligation to disclose basic financial information.

People and institutions that interact with firms are gaining unprecedented access to all sorts of information about corporate behavior, operations, and performance. Armed with new tools to find information about matters that affect their interests, all sorts of stakeholders now scrutinize the firm like never before, informing others and organizing collective responses. The corporation is becoming naked.

Customers can evaluate the worth of products and services at levels not possible before. Employees share formerly secret information about corporate strategy, management, and challenges. To collaborate effectively, companies and their business partners have no choice but to share intimate knowledge with one another. Powerful institutional investors today own or manage most wealth, and they are developing x-ray vision. Finally, in a world of instant communications, whistleblowers, inquisitive media, and Googling, citizens and communities routinely put firms under the microscope. Corporations have no choice but to rethink their values and behaviors – for the better. If you're going to be naked, you'd better be buff! By that we mean you'd better have the best value (as value is evidenced like never before) but you'd also better have values – of honesty, accountability, consideration of others' interests, and openness – built into your corporate DNA, operations, and systems. Otherwise, you will be unable to build trust and a sustainable business.

This conclusion may seem at odds with current thinking about corporate values and behavior. At the end of 2003, the corporate world was still weathering a crisis of trust on a scale unseen since the Wall Street crash of 1929. Many say this latest crisis proves that companies are worse than ever, and irredeemably so. For these critics, the corporate corpus isn't buff, it's obese.

Our research shows the opposite is true. To build trusting relationships and succeed in a transparent economy, growing numbers of firms in all parts of the globe now behave more responsibly than ever. Disgraced firms represent the old model – a dying breed. Business integrity is on the rise, not just for legal or purely ethical reasons, but because it makes economic sense. Firms that exhibit ethical values, openness, and candor have discovered that they can better compete and profit. Some figured this out recently, while others have understood it for generations. Today's winners increasingly undress for success. Of course, opacity is still alive and kicking; in some situations it remains desirable and necessary. Trade secrets and personal data, for example, are properly kept confidential. Sometimes openness is expensive. But more often, opacity is used only to mask deeper problems. Armies of corporate lawyers fight openness as part of a good day's work. Old cultures – the insular model of yesterday's firm – die hard. Nevertheless, the technological, economic, and sociopolitical drivers of an open business world will prevail. Corporations that are open perform better. Transparency is a new form of power, which pays off when harnessed. Rather than to be feared, transparency is becoming central to business success. Rather than to be unwillingly stripped, smart firms are choosing to be open. Over time, open enterprises – firms that operate with candor, integrity, and engagement – are most likely to survive and thrive. The best firms have clear leadership practices that others can adopt. They understand that investments in good governance and transparency deliver significant payoffs: engaged relationships, better quality and cost management, more innovation, and improved overall business performance. They build transparency and integrity into their business strategy, products and services, brand and reputation, technology plans and corporate character. They share pertinent information and build trust and stronger relationships with employees, customers, shareholders, business partners, community members, and other interest groups. Increasingly firms now want to be seen as honest, accountable, considerate, and transparent, but each of these characteristics requires a supportive IT strategy.

Maturation

Detractors like to point out that IT is just like other technologies that started out as arcane and proprietary (an example, of course, is electricity), but then became standardized and commoditized. The trend in IT has been for this process to happen higher and higher in the "stack," from RS232C for electrical signaling (for example), to Cobol, to standard application programs like Word. The value of standards is widely recognized today, and often the speed of standardization is quite rapid (802.11 being a good example).

One great advantage of standards is the ability to link disparate objects through a standard interface. Web services and related technologies are attempts to allow applications in the extended enterprise to be "compiled" from a high-level description of the functions they perform, which is translated either once, or even dynamically, into invocation of existing services/objects. This is isomorphic with the functional view of the Enterprise 2.0, and the more rapidly such technologies mature, the more rapidly will the Enterprise 2.0 be realized as a standard organizational form.

Information in cyberspace

The traditional enterprise (even the firm in a b-web) could think of itself, its customers, suppliers, and competitors as elements related dyadically – e.g., the firm vis-à-vis its customers, in a sales relationship – without worrying too much about a third significant – and independent – element. This element is the mass of information located in cyberspace. It cannot readily be controlled by the firm, with the result that previously simple relationships can become fundamentally reshaped.

As we have said, the consumer becomes empowered through the availability of information on the Web and the existence of various infomediaries who aggregate this information. The focus in this analysis is on the power shift in the dyadic relationship between the firm and its customers. Now enter Google. Google may be thought of as a means for the consumer to get better information (and it is). But the Google model of today (and those of its equally effective competitors) is not to make it easier to find information, but to monetize the case where the information found is part of a potential commercial transaction. Google may even be interested in providing VoIP services in the event that a consumer calls a supplier Google has identified. For some kinds of suppliers (so-called "long-tail" sellers) Google is a market maker, and an essential player in their sales. Enterprise 2.0 networks will in many cases include Google (or Yahoo!, or another competitor).

Collaboration technologies

As I explained earlier, new forms of collaboration are reshaping the firm. Open innovation via innovation webs offer one example, where the open-source model is emulated in the creation of various kinds of intellectual property, and, concomitantly, various ways of compensating the firm that orchestrates such innovation. Many of the new collaboration technologies provide ways to filter and reduce the vast amount of information on the Web, by such means as collaborative filtering.

It is striking that much of the innovation in collaboration technology has its roots outside commercial applications: good examples are wikis, instant messaging, blogs, RSS feeds, and podcasting. Such tools are revitalizing the knowledge management arena and helping firms leverage their human capital more effectively, even though their first application was in more general social networking. Note that these immensely powerful tools can be created quite trivially. In contrast to the difficulty attending the creation of an application like Lotus Notes, an application like Flickr (a social networking program for sharing digital images) can be cobbled together very rapidly using today's scripting languages. To summarize, as exponential growth in capability forces IT into many more non-corporate domains, it is no longer adequate to look just at the co-evolution of the firm and IT. Instead we must look at the nature of computer use in quite different environments, such as entertainment and social networking, where technology is evolving more rapidly, and watch out for emergent phenomena like Google and the blogosphere where the nature of the Enterprise 2.0 could be redefined.

The Enterprise 2.0: rethinking business strategy

Information technology never conferred competitive advantage other than the changes to information and businesses it enabled. But as we see a new paradigm in technology emerging, combined with new demands of the global business environment, IT is becoming more important than ever in enabling better information and powerful new business processes, designs, and strategies. All the evidence points to the startling fact that we are at an inflection point in economic history, as the corporation – the institution of wealth creation in all societies – is changing fundamentally. If the corporation is changing, then so are the requirements for strategy. Strategy is about being different or better than competitors. But in this new environment some new perspectives are emerging, among them:

- Business designs and architectures are the new foundation of strategy. The old corporation was a tractor on the race track. The Enterprise 2.0 is the business model equivalent of a race car – build it and you can win. Make the right boundary and partnering choices and remake them, continuously.

- Embrace the themes of the Enterprise 2.0. Evaluate where you stand today on each and intensify the work of migrating on each. For every company, at least a few of these will require radical rethinking of the way firms innovate, collaborate, compete, and are managed.

- Strategy is more than competitiveness. In a world of infinite business designs and possibilities, previously inconceivable opportunities to create new value will emerge. There was no competitor to the RIM Blackberry or iTunes/iPod experience. They started with a customer value proposition and built the b-webs to deliver. Having said that, both face fierce competition today. This insight leads to the next point.

- Strategy is more than execution. The post dot-com, post recession world demands that firms think about innovation and growth. Execution is a necessary but insufficient condition for success.

- Sustainable advantage may well be an oxymoron. The pace of innovation, fast-track business models and numerous other factors evaluated in this research mean that most forms of market advantage will be copied or undercut, eventually. The solution is vigilance, agility, capability development, and sustained competitive innovation.

- In the open, networked world, strategy is not a linear exercise. There are fewer cause-and-effect linkages. Think of strategy as a system in which the outcomes depend not only on your actions, but on the actions of competitors as well – it is a dynamic system with non-linear outcomes. You must engage in systems that you do not fully control.

- Increasingly, many components of IT are commoditized and will be available through the "utility" or infrastructure available to many firms. Companies should exploit such opportunities to reduce IT costs, while shifting investments to areas that really matter.

If the emerging model of the enterprise represents a new paradigm, be prepared for a leadership crisis. As I have argued before, new paradigms cause uncertainty and are often received with coolness or worse. Vested interests fight change and leaders of the old are often the last to embrace the new. What is your role in providing leadership for these changes?

This article is excerpted from a report delivered to New Paradigm clients as part of the „Winning with the Enterprise 2.0" syndicated research project. (c) New Paradigm 2007.

WORKS CITED

Drucker, Peter (1988): The Coming of the New Organization. In: Harvard Business Review. January-February 66 (1), pp. 45-53.

Drucker, Peter (1989): The New Realities in Government and Politics / In Economics and Business / In Society and World View. 1st ed. New York.

Saint-Onge, Hubert (2005): Collaborative Knowledge and Competitive Advantage. New Paradigm, IT & CA Big Idea Series.

Tapscott, Don (1996): The Digital Economy. Promise and Peril in the Age of Networked Intelligence. New York.

Tapscott, Don/Ticoll, David (2005): The Naked Corporation: How the Age of Transparency Will Revolutionize Business. Free Press.

Tapscott, Don/Warner, Tim (2005): The Shifting Context of Business, New Paradigm, IT & CA Big Idea Series.

Ticoll, David/Hood, Phil (2005): The Dancing Penguin: Harnessing Self-Organization for Competitive Advantage, New Paradigm, IT & CA Big Idea Series.

Willms Buhse
Beauty Comes from Within: The New Culture of Communication in Enterprise 2.0

A new culture of communication for openness and clarity

As early as the 1980s, media philosopher Vilem Flusser was describing the societal consequences of the media society – which he dubbed the "telematic society" – pointing to the dangers of missing out on the opportunities offered by these new media forms. For Flusser, the way that the new media overcame spatial distances opened up new avenues of freedom. In his vision of society, new information is constantly being created, based on the free flow of dialog via digital media. The established authorities on opinion and information disappear, replaced by a networked structure that cybernetically decides its own direction.

Today, the power of networking – the cornerstone of Flusser's vision – can be experienced by everyone. Cell phones represent the development of a swarm culture, which can rapidly change shape and organize itself into groups. Agreements and planned goals are temporary – since third-party contacts can take place at practically any time, and from any location. The capability to accept and actuate rapid change is vital, as is the ability to quickly reorient oneself to face new competitive challenges and changes in business processes. All members of such a swarm are constantly in possession of the current state of information, monitoring incoming messages and adapting accordingly. Would you like an example from the Web 2.0 world?

Already twittering? Twitter can be defined as "microblogging": the aim being to answer the simple question "What are you doing?" with a simple snippet of text. Such snippets consist of a maximum of 140 characters, such as may be received via SMS from other users, for example. Service users decide who they would like to receive texts from, and who they want to send their own messages to. The result is a mixture of information exchange, social networking and entertainment.[18] The newly-acquired freedom of movement ups the tempo, while the high degree of networking lends flexibility, giving the swarm a new direction.

Such communicative experiences also apply to the Internet. This is one of the reasons why Internet usage has risen from nine minutes a day in 1996 to 72 minutes at present – while the time spent on TV, radio and newsprint has remained unchanged. The PC is telephone, photo album, DVD player and playground, as well as a platform for sharing, flirts or encounters. It inspires interaction and participation and encourages self-promotion on the Internet itself or via MySpace or Facebook profiles, personal videos on YouTube, or via other communities, blogs and forums.

Everyone's networked with everyone else. Anything that can be digitized is. If it can be done directly or decentralized, then it is. The Net makes markets and companies more open and also a little more democratic. Internet users enjoy not just a vast array of opportunities, but also great power. Is it time to call it quits for classical advertising? The purpose and methodology of marketing has certainly been radically altered by increased networking and its associated openness.

Web 2.0 is the motto for this paradigm shift. What implications does this increased openness have for marketing? Is the "art of letting go" a real alternative for marketing managers in an era in which analysts never tire of pointing out that between 30% and 90% of company value is attributable to its communication strategies?[19]

Enterprise 2.0 – New challenges for marketing

Markets are (once again) a conversation

"Markets are conversations": the slogan of Levine, Locke, Searls and Weinberger in their *Cluetrain Manifesto*, published in 1999 as the first Internet tidal wave of the New Economy plunged the world temporarily into a progressive frenzy. The Internet created a new forum for conversations: the network allows personal encounters to be essentially unlimited. Here, communities can communicate with one another, discuss and form opinions at breakneck speed. Such discussions are not constrained by time and place. The new media technologies change the rules of the game: they create previously-unknown rates of acceleration and dynamism, multiplying interactions and increasing the degree of networking to such an extent that they change the very culture of collaboration. The Internet by its very nature provides the technical background for the presentation, documentation and organization of processes for dialog and discussion, setting up networks supporting communication that integrates cultural norms.

Traditional lines of demarcation between staff, external partners and customers begin to blur, with multiple partners working in varying roles within projects, independently of organizational structures and unheeding of natural boundaries such as national borders or time zones. At the same time, shortened product lifecycles require rapid and flexible decisionmaking so that new portfolios of products and services can be brought to market. Companies that learn faster are more innovative. Inflexible, hierarchical structures for communication and organization seem to be doomed to extinction in such an environment.

Web 2.0 itself is a watershed in the continual process of change that digital media technologies have brought about in business and society. The Internet generation is finding new ways of collaborating with the networked enterprises of the future. The key asset for this new kind of company consists of digital media technologies whose versatile structures for communication and organization can network staff, customers and partners with one another. Andrew McAfee, Associate Professor of the Harvard Business School, has coined the term "Enterprise 2.0" to describe this new kind of company.

An "Enterprise 2.0" provides its staff with Web 2.0 technologies, letting them communicate and collaborate freely and directly not only with their colleagues, but also with business partners and customers. In this new world, internal and external boundaries disappear: Web 2.0 grants each and every individual member of staff unfettered access to the outside world.

Survey results: marketing and Enterprise 2.0

Within German companies, the subject of Web 2.0 is still in its infancy, according to the findings of a study commissioned from Berlecon Research[20] by CoreMedia. The study reports that the subject is most actively promulgated by marketing departments: 56 percent of marketing management staff are convinced that Web 2.0 applications will be part of corporate daily business in just a few years. However, only a quarter of all marketing management staff describe their current IT infrastructure as adequate.

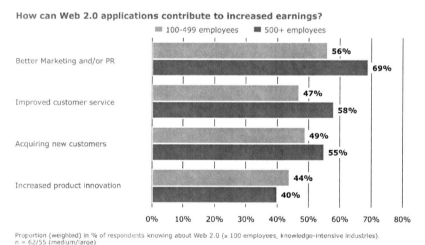

How can Web 2.0 applications contribute to increased earnings?

Proportion (weighted) in % of respondents knowing about Web 2.0 (≥ 100 employees, knowledge-intensive industries). n = 62/55 (medium/large)

Figure 1: Respondents from major corporations with more than 500 employees believe that Web 2.0 applications can help increase turnover.

Apart from company management and IT departments, 48 percent of respondents from major corporations view marketing in particular as being a driving force behind the introduction of Web 2.0 applications. Can those of us in marketing rise to the challenge of being the driving force behind this paradigm shift?

The evolution of marketing

The question of what influence the increasing connectivity of Enterprise 2.0 has on marketing goes hand in hand with these purely empirical findings. It helps to look back briefly into the 150-year history of marketing itself.

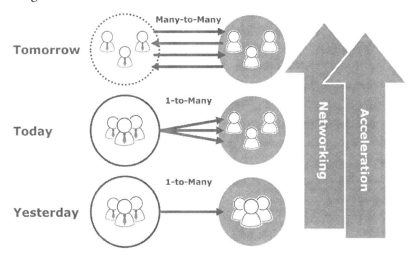

Figure 2: The previously clear lines of demarcation within the corporation are disappearing. In Enterprise 2.0, marketing has to learn to deal with acceleration, networking and transparency.

Methods of communication originated in open dialog within markets. Up until the 19th century, the market was not only a trading center but also an environment for open dialog between producers and consumers. Selling points were shouted out, before being discussed by the customer and the seller personally. Around the turn of the century, the first branded products jostled for attention on store shelves. As mass markets and mass production were established, producers lost the direct line of communication with their consumers and competition increased significantly. Marketing assumed the role of the silent seller and, at the same time, direct consumer feedback was lost.

By the time of the post-war economic boom, marketing had established itself worldwide as a branch of corporate activity concerned with external communication using the "one-to-many" principle: a single person spoke from on high down to the many consumers below, with early marketing pioneers sending simple messages into an abstract mass market. Marketing began to deal with this abstract mass market by relying on a high degree of segmentation, culminating in the approach of addressing individual consumers directly (one-to-one marketing). Marketing was quick to understand the advantages of the Internet: the ability to address the customer directly, supported by technology that offered greater precision, speed, cost-efficiency and interaction than ever before. And yet, while more direct and more accurately targeted at a particular individual, the principle remained the same: the sender of the message remained a monolithic company, firing off a single message into the mass of consumers. Even today, marketing is still seen as a function that integrates and thus controls: a department that formulates and "authorizes" the company's message, before introducing it into the market to generate attention.

Yet the business culture of the digital economy also increases marketing's complexity. Those in marketing management have lost their authority over media channels – in a way similar to developments in the media industry. Users are increasingly gaining the upper hand, unforgiving in their selection of what they want to watch and read. As David Weinberger correctly states: "respect the conversation – it belongs to your customers."[21]

Therefore, providers must recognize their users' needs and get the users involved interactively. Conventional marketing messages are quickly exposed as manipulation and thus miss their mark – indeed, they occasionally provoke the exact opposite of what the message intended. One example is the creation of promotional blogs by authors who are in fact working for the company's PR agency. Another is the story of the blogger who showed how the allegedly "secure" bicycle locks made by

Kryptonite could be opened with a ballpoint pen – and posted videos to prove it: ensuing events demonstrate well how companies can still be in denial about the immediate effects of the new communications platforms. The company's PR department initially attempted to play down the problem for a few days. To little or no effect, as it subsequently turned out: the end result was a nearly 40 percent drop in turnover combined with considerable damage to the company's reputation.[22]

"Web 2.0 makes it hard for companies to lie. The new participative Internet culture means that each and every tiny transgression will be found out sooner or later. Those who are tempted to bend the rules must reckon with serious consequences – up to and including the total loss of company reputation."[23] The above statement may also be taken to apply to communication within the company, too – as recent examples from Siemens, Volkswagen or Deutsche Telekom have shown us only too well.

Marketing challenges in Enterprise 2.0

The old companies and brands that spoke to their customers as anonymous, abstract institutions will become mixed communities of employees, partners and customers, where marketing will need to take on the role of matchmaker between staff and the outside world. For marketing, this marks a return to the origins of business and commerce: the direct contact between supplier and consumer, a many-to-many marketing model. Enterprise 2.0 thus requires a fast-moving, versatile marketing team, which cultivates the intimate involvement of the company with its public, promotes dialog and actively brings external stimuli into the enterprise. Rather than hindering openness and clarity, marketing must promote these principles. What then are the challenges that confront marketing in Enterprise 2.0?

Conventional marketing processes such as briefings, copywriting and authorization are too slow for many markets. How can marketing keep pace with the market itself? Can marketing achieve „real-time"?

Many traditional marketing messages miss their mark, since they seem artificial and hardly authentic – mere company rhetoric about its own supposed advantages. Marketing's self-aggrandizement frequently lacks even the support of the company's own staff. Who has not heard a member of sales retort, "Yes, I know, that's what the marketing brochure says."? How can marketing make its messages so authentic that they are accepted?

No generation has ever communicated so widely and through so many different channels as the current Internet generation. How can marketing utilize these forces for the benefit of the enterprise? How can the missing feedback channel from the market be reinstated?

People make marketing

"The strongest motivation in human nature is the desire to be important."
John Dewey

The gap between interest and belief in the possibilities offered by Web 2.0 and the inadequate support provided by IT leads one to suspect that Enterprise 2.0 is about much more than just technology. The deciding factor is the people, the staff of a company, since they not only determine how technology is employed but also shape the corporate culture. It is often overlooked that the „digital natives" – the kids who have not known a world without the Internet – are now beginning their careers as high potentials. These new members of staff are used to unhindered communication over the Internet. They send instant messages, install software themselves and sign up for online services. Yet in corporate life they are offered a place to work where it takes days to get a password, where email accounts are limited to 5 MB storage, and where the employer flatly denies them Internet access.

Companies that promulgate such rules will not attract any high potential candidates: instead of enhancing their growth, they will face extinction, since fast-paced networking is a chief characteristic of business in the media society. Those who learn faster than others gain a competitive advantage. Jack Welch, Chairman and CEO of General Electric from 1981-2001, recognized this necessity early on: "An organization's ability to learn, and translate that learning into action rapidly, is the ultimate competitive advantage."

This is just one of the reasons why we should ensure that we give our staff members exactly the same freedoms with regard to technology that they have become used to in their private lives. The role model for our cultural evolution is an Enterprise 2.0 – a communicative company that listens well, learns fast and is creative in realizing its ideas. This role model exemplifies self-organization, teamwork, projects and innovations – lots of movement, minimal control, with confusion and discord on occasion.

The Internet is a giant stage, where many people from the Internet generation are now jockeying for their share of public recognition. Marketing in Enterprise 2.0 acts within the company, both utilizing and cultivating employees' appetite for prestige. Enterprise 2.0 marketing motivates all employees to speak and write about their work, their insights and their accomplishments – without fear of censorship. Many companies take the plunge by starting with a CEO blog – as have Jonathan Schwartz[24], CEO and President of Sun Microsystems, or Bob Lutz[25], Vice Chairman of General Motors. At the beginning of 2006, GM was in crisis, announcing factory closures and the shedding of 30,000 jobs. At that time, Lutz asked for assistance on his blog: "We need to step up our non-traditional communications and word of mouth, and get our message directly to the people on a grass roots level. […] What do you think?" To date there have been around 350 answers from customers and staff members on topics such as longer warranty periods, the product range, etc.

The BMW corporation records ad hoc interviews with staff members and posts these online. One interview might be with the telematics project leader, the next with the head of engine development. Indeed, video articles starring the head of engine development were watched 2.5 million times. Production costs were €40,000 for 37 videos.[26]

Daimler also hosts staff blogs – somewhat unassuming and yet highly personal – at http://blog.daimler.de/. There, staff post on subjects such as career, society, the company, its products, innovation and sustainability. An excerpt: "On Wednesday, December 5, 2007, I got involved in the 'An Honor to Participate' project, where you volunteer to work for a good cause. My mommy works at DaimlerChrysler Bank in Stuttgart as Information Technology Management Secretary."

Figure 3: http://blog.daimler.de/hier-bloggen-mitarbeiter/

Other examples include a product blog from Schweppes[27], a customer service blog at FRoSTA[28], and a crisis blog from Dell, covering the subject of overheating batteries.[29]

Participation encourages motivation. Therefore, all staff should be given the chance to continually involve themselves in current processes or in the development and promotion of ideas. Their opinions – even critical ones – should be heard. An open discussion process paves the way for decisionmaking and also builds trust: a participative corporate culture empowers all staff members to develop themselves personally while exchanging their individual know-how.

How then can our talented colleagues now become part of innovative communities?

The corporate Social Network

Social networks are currently in vogue on the Internet, whether business communities such as Xing or LinkedIn or student communities such as StudiVZ and (originally) Facebook. There are also communities for soccer fans (fussball.de), architects (designerpages.com) or wine aficionados (mycellar.de). Ning and wirsind.de now even let people easily build their own private label communities. What significance do communities have for companies?

Corporate communities create both strong ties (explicit connections) and weak ties (group affiliations)[30] between staff members, facilitate inter-departmental contact and international collaboration between branch offices, and help identify the experts on a particular subject. One example of a starting point for an internal community is IBM's BluePages – the expansion of their internal directory services.

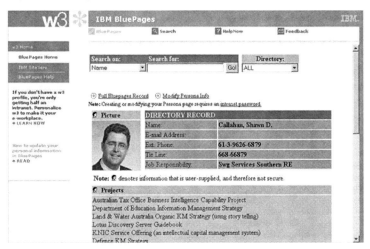

Figure 4: www.research.ibm.com

A vision of how this service might develop further is an application that also shows internal relationships via functions such as person tagging, testimonials and group lists.[31]

Figure 5: www.research.ibm.com

Companies have now freed themselves of the constraints of time and place. It's no longer the location, department or company affiliation that determines the capacity for collaboration, but instead, a shared set of common interests and values. The success of Enterprise 2.0 is not entirely dependent on a technical infrastructure, but more crucially on the ability to make active use of the informal network of staff, partners and customers that exists in any company. In Enterprise 2.0, the lines between members of staff, partners and customers begin to blur.

How then do you manage communication when change is the watchword? How can you cope with extremely short-term planning cycles? How can you keep people informed about subjects that are under continual development? For example, since CoreMedia places great value on personal relationships between staff and customers, partners and end-users, our marketing concentrates on staging events that foster personal encounters while initiating and stimulating discussions.

In the process, CoreMedia's social network grows outward from the inside: from the socially-competent individual to the staff team, through to the interdisciplinary staff-partner-customer team. The goal is a social network of customers, partners and staff members who utilize their groups to make contact, maintain relationships and exchange ideas and expertise. We call it the "CoreMunity".

And marketing sees itself as the platform manager for CoreMunity. Apart from events, the central element of our company-wide dialog is our community platform "CoCo".

The enterprise community platform CoCo: initial experiences

First the people, then the technology. In the past, technologies that support knowledge and information management in the enterprise have often been notorious for the problems they experienced with unsatisfactory corporate user acceptance and the associated lack of appreciable uptake. Yet widespread usage and a broad user base are crucial to the efficient employment of knowledge management and collaboration solutions. As CoreMedia developed its Enterprise 2.0 platform in steps, it was thus able to test on itself the significance of corporate culture in the introduction of such a system.

The cornerstone of CoreMedia's infrastructure is the CoCo online platform, whose blog forums witness a constant dialog between staff, customers and partners. Conversations that arise from face-to-face encounters are resumed online. The space is used to document events and to initiate and continue discussions. In CoCo's public and private communities, partners and IT managers converse with CoreMedia experts on topics such as deployment, operations and tuning, editors talk about processes and usability, and decisionmakers discuss the opportunities and risks related to Enterprise 2.0. The continual dialog concerning requirements and technical possibilities generates both ideas and expertise for innovations. The decisive factor here is the speed with which direct feedback can be given. These rapid feedback loops not only enable the networking of experts that share common ground, but at the same time boosts the company's capacity to learn.

Each author decides who may or may not read his or her postings. Each and every article can be allocated a particular level of privacy: these privacy levels determine whether a posting can be read only by fellow colleagues, or by members of a closed user group (such as partners or customers, for example), or by any and all visitors to the CoCo online platform. The only guideline is one I myself offered, namely: "Don't write anything stupid."

Figure 6: CoCo – open dialog with staff, partners and customers

For improved networking and services, the following technical requirements can be recommended for Enterprise 2.0 software:

- Rich user profiles

- Single-sign-on (via OpenID or Facebook, for example)

- Community features for intranet, extranet and Internet – such as blogs, discussion forums and wiki capabilities

- Content management, shared workspaces and documents

- Audio and video, e.g. corporate TV, podcasts

- Social tags and social bookmarking

- Direct feedback (via recommendations, comments and ratings)

- Notifications, email integration and workflows (e.g. for external approval processes)

- Content feeds and syndication via RSS

- Voting and collaborative filtering

- Staff search, full-text content search

- Expert search plus reputation management

- Analysis and reporting capability

- Security-related features such as role-based access control and encryption at the content level

The advantages of the online platform are apparent on several levels:

- Each area of the company automatically has access to the same status of information on current issues. Interested and affected parties can team up more rapidly and enter into direct communication. Creativity and quality develop.

- Experts can respond directly concerning their specialist topics, open queries are clarified more speedily and information is made available to each and every user. Internal knowledge becomes more transparent.

- Insights – and hence innovations – are implemented more rapidly company-wide. The company becomes more streamlined and increases its competitiveness.

- All staff members and all specialist departments are in step with one another within the company's immediate environment. Focus on market and customers improves.

This is all very well, of course, but what role is then left for marketing in an environment where the majority of the daily communication work is already undertaken by members of staff? Well, as with so many things in life, it starts at the top – with marketing management.

From marketing management to coaching

Communication processes that are overly functional or technocratic will be unable to fully unlock the potential of Enterprise 2.0, since the latter depends heavily on how easily people can interconnect and how flexible they are in responding to short-term changes. Accordingly, marketing in Enterprise 2.0 dispenses with hierarchical, rigidly-structured organizational models and concentrates instead on realizing the full potential of "soft" factors such as creativity, people skills and versatility. In Enterprise 2.0, management reduces the incidence of subject-specific directives, reasoning that isolated decisions made by individual managers cannot hope to encompass the complexity and dynamism of the new marketing requirements. Only the collaborative efforts of experts from diverse disciplines acting in concert will produce decisions that satisfy all of the requirements – whether concerning content, design or technology.

Active within the company, marketing management also organizes topics and events for external communication while promoting direct dialog with its target audiences, which include not only customers, partners and staff but also journalists and analysts.

The interdisciplinary nature of collaboration between a multitude of experts requires a management style that enables decisions at the group level while creating an atmosphere of trust. Accordingly, marketing management at CoreMedia dedicates itself to the task of promoting people skills, teamwork and the general empowerment of staff members.

External staff – whether Advertising Agencies, PR consultants, copywriters or designers – are fully integrated into the marketing team. They make individual contributions, bringing their specific know-how into the team process. The integration of external specialists and internal staff members has brought flexibility and speed into our marketing processes. As a result, CoreMedia's current marketing team operates more as an innovative agency for technology marketing than as a traditional marketing department.

The management team intervenes in marketing decisions about content or planning only under exceptional circumstances. Instead, management work focuses on supporting the expert teams with coaching and feedback. Management promotes the talents and self-reliance of team members, helps with conflict resolution and gives feedback on results, performance and priorities.

Is this the "art of letting go"?

Control: losing it and getting it back

The focus on technically-enabled one-to-one marketing has made it easy to measure results. Never before could we react and maneuver so quickly. If our thesis is correct – that optimal networking can catapult companies into pole position in their industry – then it is important to understand what "optimal" means in networking terms and how this can best be achieved. Is this perhaps where the future of marketing management lies?

In sociology, network density is defined by a parameter that describes the relationship between people's actual contacts in a social network and the sum total of their possible contacts within the same network. Since the work of Elizabeth Bott, it is assumed that greater network density equates to increased mutual social answerability. Thus: higher network densities lead to greater improvements in self-organization and personal accountability.

Bernardo Huberman[32], Argentinian network researcher, departmental head at Hewlett Packard and author of the book "The Laws of the Web" used email spectroscopy to reveal the workings of the internal networks at HP. Huberman's team fed their analysis systems with email traffic from around 500 colleagues. Admins had been logging both recipient and sender for a total of two months. After a few hours of number-crunching, Huberman's servers were able to identify the informal networks at HP. Information hubs came to light, which were frequently the targets of mail as well as "communities of practice": groups that communicate a lot but which do not necessarily belong to the same department. Commenting on the results, Huberman notes that "email spectroscopy enables us to automatically locate teams and leaders in their field." Companies with several thousand employees could similarly find out if their organizational chart really does reflect the current work relationships within the company.

Truly, a management dream come true! How can these insights be utilized for the development of an Enterprise 2.0 company? And what happens when companies can scientifically establish the degree to which they are networked and able to accurately assess to what degree their employees are networked with one another and with the wider world? Do key indicators such as the contacts in Xing or Facebook, blog postings and comments now suddenly have a leading role to play in the future viability of a company?[33]

Summary: beauty comes from within

The new media are radically changing the speed and efficiency of communication as well as the degree to which it is networked. They require an approach to marketing that appreciates how the Internet empowers openness – one that involves staff, customers and partners and also dispenses with strict controls. Marketing is active within the company and motivates staff to engage in external dialog. Put another way: the new media necessitate the art of letting go – reducing strict controls and boosting trust. The illusion of marketing "controlling" markets must be dismissed: instead, staff must be encouraged to enter into direct contact with the market. The study from Berlecon and CoreMedia cited above has clearly made the case that the responsibility lies with marketing management: they need to be the catalyst for this change.

Communications media are no longer passive, but are interactive tools for the production of personal content – and not only in one's private life, but also in the workplace. Instead of presenting the brand via standard messages, marketing should instead encourage staff to produce and publish creative and authentic statements themselves. Marketing must communicate more strongly inwards than outwards while positioning staff, partners and customers as the ambassadors of the company. And not forgetting that in a networked and thus more open world, home truths are more likely to reach the public ear. Lies will get you nowhere fast. Once the company is no longer shrouded by marketing, it operates virtually "naked" in the public sphere. And, as has been observed: "If you're naked, you'd better be in shape."[34] Or, as the German saying goes: "Beauty comes from within."

Therefore, in an Enterprise 2.0 company, marketing supplies the company's social network with an infrastructure that networks the company and the outside world, while creating openness and ensuring that all participants act together in concert. Are these thoughts merely utopian or do they constitute a realistic vision? One might also posit the question that this kind of networked communication might work well in a relatively small company such as CoreMedia, but is not applicable to major corporations. And of course, these new strategies must observe existing guidelines such as the stock corporation act, co-determination laws or work agreements. The risks should also not be underestimated: via blogs, staff members will begin to inform the public about technical, organizational and even personal details – content that may even be sensitive information about the company. On the other hand, if frustrated staff really want to denounce their own company, then they will find other ways of doing it even if none are offered. The ultimate cause of this unrest is hardly likely to be a blogging platform, but instead dissatisfaction with the way they have been treated in the past.

My experience tells me that the preparation for this paradigm shift begins in the mind – and has already been completed in the minds of many younger colleagues.

Perhaps it is best to start things off with a few of the company's best communicators, perhaps even initially including approval processes, thus enabling a step-by-step opening-up of the company. In the future, no company will be able to dispense with optimally utilizing employees' energy in the form of personal recommendations and the expression of opinions. One authentic blog posting can have a far greater effect than a press release or a conventional advertising campaign could achieve. Personal opinions invite discussion and feedback – and have the power to change the world.

Nicole Dufft
Reality Check Enterprise 2.0: The State of Play within German Companies

Problem outline

Web 2.0 is currently one of the most common buzzwords within ITC. While the initial euphoria concentrated on media and entertainment services for young consumers, the ideas behind Web 2.0 are now being discussed increasingly in a business context, where it is known as "Enterprise 2.0." This is understandable, since wikis, blogs, social networks, and the like offer significant potential for both efficient and versatile knowledge management and for collaboration within and between companies. Importantly, the innovative character of the Enterprise 2.0 principle reveals itself not only in the use of new technologies, but also – even primarily – in the new approaches taken, and in the changes made to corporate culture.

While many Enterprise 2.0 concepts are not entirely new, they are currently enjoying something of a heyday. The reason is clear: companies today know that they are facing drastically altered conditions in the global marketplace – conditions for which the old ways of collaborating or exchanging knowledge and information are not entirely suitable. In the current climate, information and knowledge have to be used both rapidly and flexibly to create innovation, independently of any rigid organizational structure. In product development, for example, it is increasingly common for global teams to work together on a project, regardless of whether their market role is partner, competitor, or client. In such an environment, Enterprise 2.0 principles enable companies to thrive, letting them access data efficiently, process content dynamically, connect a multitude of partners (both internal and external to the company), and tap into previously undiscovered sources of knowledge.

However, in the midst of all this excitement, one question does need to be asked: does company management understand the opportunities presented by Enterprise 2.0 for meeting these new challenges? Do the decision-makers believe that they will be able to optimize their company-internal processes with the help of Web 2.0 applications – and that collaboration, knowledge management, and information sharing will become more efficient? And to what extent are they already using tools such as blogs, wikis, social networks, or social bookmarking?

In order to be able to answer these questions with more than merely anecdotal evidence, CoreMedia commissioned Berlecon Research to conduct a representative survey in the summer of 2007 that would cover the usage and appraisal of Web 2.0 within German corporations. The survey asked 156 senior management personnel, employed at companies in 'knowledge-intensive'[35] industries with more than 100 members of staff.

These industries were chosen because of their pressing need for efficient knowledge and information management, which also means that the potential for introducing Enterprise 2.0 in these companies is especially high. Interviews were computer-supported, over-the-phone dialogues, with management personnel from R&D, Marketing, Public Relations, and Human Resources being asked for their opinions on the following topics:[36]

What are the current key challenges within the company regarding teamwork and the exchange of knowledge and information? How have these challenges evolved during the last few years?

What is the company position with regard to the relevance and benefit of Web 2.0 applications?

How extensive is the use of Web 2.0 applications, and which reasons are given for not using these tools within the company?

What are the driving forces within the company for the implementation of Web 2.0 concepts and technologies?

Current challenges

The survey results serve to confirm the general thesis that companies must act now to change the ways and means by which they communicate and collaborate if they are to have a chance of facing up to the new challenges. Nearly 90 percent of the respondents say that they have experienced an increased demand for efficient teamwork and knowledge transfer in recent years; two-thirds of all respondents go as far as to say that demand has increased strongly. At the same time, less than half of the technical departmental heads questioned felt that they were being sufficiently supported in meeting this demand by their company's provisioning of ICT.

One of the most serious problems for respondents is dealing with immense quantities of often irrelevant information. For example, the excessive use of e-mail systems often leads to employees being 'snowed under' by unimportant information (see Figure 1).

Assessing the relevance of available information (as stored on the intranet, for example) was also deemed problematic, in the absence of tools for rating or recommending content.

On the other hand, the challenge arising from the need to more strongly integrate knowledge produced by staff, customers, or partners for the benefit of the company receives minimal consideration. Only a comparatively small percentage of respondents believe that the knowledge and ideas of partners and customers or of staff members is being under-exploited within their company (see Figure 1). Thus it seems that one of the core principles of Web 2.0 – include knowledge from as many stakeholders as possible – has not yet anchored itself within company management.

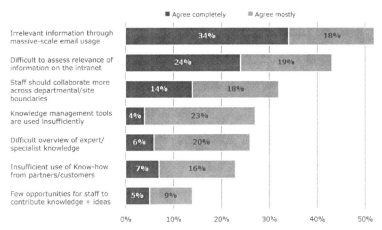

Figure 1: Challenges for companies in the exchange of knowledge and information

Relevance and extent of application of Web 2.0

The results are fairly unsurprising, given the fact that nearly a quarter of the respondents (themselves managers in key positions at major German corporations) were entirely unfamiliar with the term Web 2.0 – despite the current hype surrounding the subject. Even among those who had heard of Web 2.0, a significant minority (nearly 25 percent) consider it to be pure media hype with no business relevance.

On the other hand, around half of the respondents expect that Web 2.0 will be part of daily company business in the future. And at least a third believe that companies can utilize Web 2.0 to design their processes and collaborative systems more efficiently. These results are reassuring, since a significant proportion of our respondents recognize the relevance of Web 2.0 for business

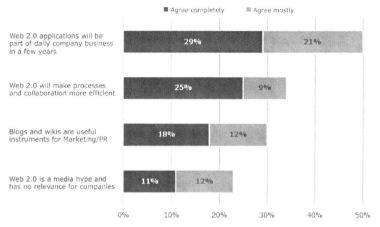

Proportion (weighted) in % of respondents knowing about Web 2.0 (≥ 100 employees, knowledge-intensive industries). n = 117-118

Figure 2: Relevance of Web 2.0 for business

However, a closer look at the actual usage of Web 2.0 applications within companies is very sobering: such tools are primarily used – if indeed at all – only by individual members of staff. Only a fraction of the companies surveyed have so far implemented Web 2.0 applications company-wide, or even across departmental boundaries (see Figure 3). By means of comparison: 70 percent of the companies have an intranet system that is provided as a company-wide service.

While it is true that a fifth of all respondents use RSS readers or social networks in their work, only 10 percent of all companies have established these as cross-department or company-wide services. Even internal blogs and wikis for staff and projects have so far rarely been implemented by the surveyed companies as services that venture outside department borders.

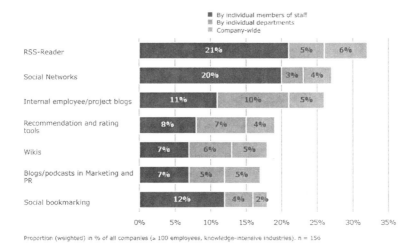

Figure 3: Web 2.0 applications in use

Yet without substantial networking support, Web 2.0 applications will not be able to reach their full potential within the business environment. As such, wikis, blogs, or social bookmarking tools will serve only to create additional knowledge silos, which then hinder rather than help the efficient use of knowledge and information. For example: if there is no possibility of conducting a search across all of the company information sources such as wikis, blogs, and knowledge management tools, then these tools will contribute little in the way of increased informational efficiency.

Assessing the usefulness of Web 2.0

The (as yet) limited experience that respondents have had with company-wide implementations of Web 2.0 tools is reflected in their assessment of the usefulness of Web 2.0 itself. Respondents view Web 2.0 applications as being most useful for locating experts and suitable contact partners, or for helping with the exchange of information (see Figure 3). This probably reflects the comparatively greater experience that the respondents have gained in their use of social network services, RSS readers, and blogs.

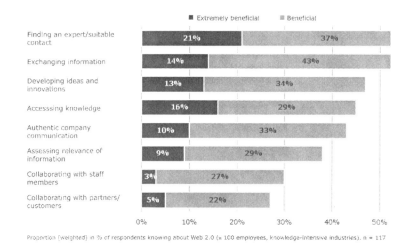

Figure 4: Benefit of Web 2.0 applications

Few respondents were of the opinion that Web 2.0 applications would help them avoid 'overload' from irrelevant information – possibly because they have not yet had any experience in this area. This is understandable, since the informational content of recommendation/rating systems or social bookmarking tools is severely limited if the majority of the workforce is not actually working with these applications on a company-wide basis.

Since there was little acknowledgment of the problems caused by failing to include knowledge from staff, customers, and partners, there were also only a few survey respondents who were of the opinion that such collaboration could be made more efficient by introducing and using Web 2.0 applications. All in all, the respondents' overall assessment reflected the fact that their experience has so far been confined to isolated, marginally networked use of Web 2.0 software.

Implementing Web 2.0: its supporters and detractors

Given this environment, one finds, unsurprisingly, that two-thirds of respondents cite the unclear business benefit of Web 2.0 as a primary reason for not introducing it into their companies. Serious security considerations or the lack of content control within Web 2.0 applications are consigned to second and third place in the list of objections to usage. Interestingly, technical complexity is placed almost last on the list of perceived barriers to usage, although it increases dramatically as network density increases within a company and differs radically from the scenario of a Web application with modest usage.

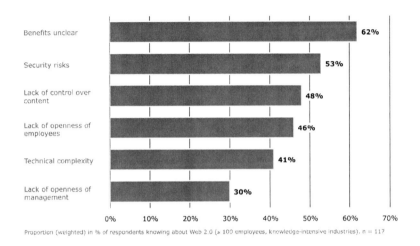

Proportion (weighted) in % of respondents knowing about Web 2.0 (≥ 100 employees, knowledge-intensive industries), n = 117

Figure 5: Reasons for rejecting Web 2.0

At present, Marketing and PR management are most often responsible for promoting Web 2.0 within German companies. They are the most important drivers for Web 2.0 usage, followed by the company executive and the IT department. This is especially true in large companies with over 500 employees, where Marketing and PR are easily the most significant driving force. Young, technology-savvy staff do not however play a dominant role here, although such a role is commonly ascribed to them when considering the introduction of new technologies into a business environment.

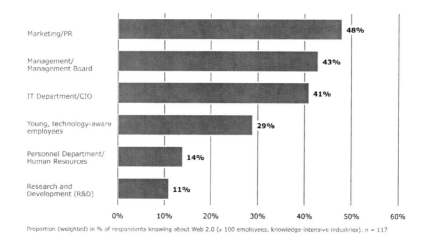

Proportion (weighted) in % of respondents knowing about Web 2.0 (≥ 100 employees, knowledge-intensive industries), n = 117

Figure 6: Which of the following groups of people were the driving force for the introduction of Web 2.0 applications within your company?

Summary

In conclusion, we identify here a development similar to that seen with the first "Internet wave" at the end of the 90s. As with the present situation, the initial euphoria then was directed chiefly at consumer services. It took a second wave to sweep the hype over into the enterprise market – a wave that was also driven initially by marketing and PR professionals. The new technologies then slowly but surely encroached on internal company processes until they became in time a normal part of our business environment.

However, it seems we have a long way to go in Germany before we reach this stage for Web 2.0. When we look at major, knowledge-intensive companies and see that a mere two to six percent use Web 2.0 tools in a company-wide fashion, then we can hardly describe these tools as "a normal part of our business environment." Moreover, without a clear perception of the usefulness of Web 2.0, a major prerequisite is missing for the spread of Enterprise 2.0 ideas within German business.

On the other hand, the broad-based opinion of respondents that Web 2.0 will be part of daily company business in the future is reassuring, since it is then only a matter of time. Sooner or later, companies will realize that their only option is to re-think the ways in which they collaborate and exchange their knowledge and information, if they are to meet the increased demands that will be made of them.

Craig Cmehil
SAP: Building Communities in the Enterprise

Many view SAP as old, closed, and opposed to innovation. A company that builds it so you have to use it. This view is wrong and it's been an adventure proving just how wrong that statement is for the last 4 years...

SAP communities of innovation

Web 2.0: a term, a phrase, a thought, an idea – which is it? It's all of that and more. It's about bringing people together to "Connect, Collaborate, and Contribute," a phrase that SAP has taken to heart and fosters through its "Communities of Innovation." The story starts in early 2003 as an idea to enable both existing and future customers to discuss aspects of the up and coming SAP NetWeaver platform. The process began with the creation of a portal for existing customers to come together, find information, and ask questions. This was the start of the SAP Developer Network (SDN). It quickly turned into a passionate community through the interaction of employees, customers, and partners. SDN was later opened to the general public as well to emphasis the idea of openness.

SDN is an active online community where ABAP, Java, .NET, and other cutting-edge technologies converge to form a resource and collaboration channel for SAP developers, consultants, integrators, and system administrators. SDN hosts a technical library, expert blogs, exclusive downloads and code samples, an extensive e-learning catalog, and active, moderated discussion forums.

SDN is a case study in success for the organic growth of a community around a specific topic. Starting small, it has expanded over four years to almost one million registered users, processes more than 5,000 daily messages and ten to twenty blog posts a week. SDN has taken advantage of the latest tools from the Web 2.0 world like forums, blogs, wikis, podcasts, and video casts to capture the communications and collaboration between community members. It also helps enable members to connect to one another through online events and virtual events, extending into real-world events.

BPX (Business Process Expert) Community provides resources to help business process experts drive real-time business process innovation. These include a rich combination of industry business process and services content and information on composition software tools from a proven business process platform, surrounded by a vibrant community of experts sharing knowledge and ideas.

The SDN community spawned the need for a new kind of community, one that caters to the specialist needs of the business process expert. This led to the development and launch of the Business Process Expert (BPX) community. SAP utilized the SDN infrastructure, elements, and services. SAP built on the learning experiences acquired through SDN development. The result was that the BPX community grew to 200,000 members in less than eighteen months. It continues to show steady growth.

Building it

The basic elements for building a community remain the same. This is a key factor many overlook, ignore, or simply refuse to accept. All communities need:

• Topic: a community is formed by the coming together of individuals who share a common interest in a specific topic area.

- Topic Expert: a community is driven by someone who clearly demonstrates topic expertise. This person provides a center of gravity, focus, and motivation to others.

- Location: every community requires a place to call their own, where they can safely meet.

- Users: location, topic, and an expert are not enough; communities need a pool of people who share the topic interest.

- Services: these are the building blocks that enable the community to communicate, collaborate, and to connect.

- Community Builder: not always required but frequently helpful when dealing with multiple communities or sub-communities. This is the individual who has an overview of services and locations and can help facilitate change across multiple communities.

The following is a brief history of the evolution of SDN and its Community Evangelists.

SDN started with a small passionate team, including Mark Finnern, its Community Builder. Mark is a visionary with a solid overview of what was happening at that the time in the SAP development world. Mark was the original driving force for the SDN community, and through his work, it began to flourish and take shape. Mark was one of the first to focus his time on supporting the top one percent of members. In any community, these are the most active, passionate members. He began to foster relationships with the one-percent crowd and discover how he could help and motivate them to continue contributing. I was one of those early enthusiasts.

At the time, I was trying to learn more about the SAP environment to help me in my work at the company where I was employed. I found that by contributing to SDN on things I did know about, my own knowledge of the SAP system increased through the comments of other developers. Developers like to solve problems, and the blogs provided a way for us to cooperate and collaborate while learning. As people saw that I was giving my knowledge, they shared their own. It was a new, fresh, and exciting experience. Mark picked up on this and shortly afterwards I became an evangelist for the community.

It was Mark's enthusiasm and passion which put me on my path of internal evangelism at my own company. My evangelizing resulted in multiple blog posts and comments within the SDN community itself regarding contests and events I had planned and executed within my own company. Fast forward to 2005. My employer decided it was time for me to move back to the US. I decided it was time to look for new opportunities and find one at SAP itself with the SDN team extending my role as an evangelist into a full-time position.

Best practices for a Community Evangelist

The following is from the "Best Practices of a Community Evangelist."

Spend thirty minutes wrapping up your day. Spend an hour browsing forums, blogs, and wiki spaces for your area. Make a note of who's who. Spend an hour surfing the external blogosphere. Spend thirty minutes on your internal team wiki spaces. Break down the other five hours of your day into two hours for write-ups, proposals, and emails, and spend three hours a day communicating and encouraging your community, maybe through t-shirt giveaways or complimenting great blog posts. Go offline somewhere in the middle of that eight hours for at least two hours. SAP has a global community, so things happen all the time. It's good to mix up your day so you can experience a different ,day' on the site.

Creating this structure is critical to maintaining both a finger on the pulse of the community as well as one's own sanity. Closing your day out with a period of reflection and understanding of what has transpired prepares you for the next day as well as reminding you of who might be the next up and coming stars to watch for. Most importantly though are "spend three hours a day communicating with your community." You need to talk to them and build a relationship. Don't simply ask them for content or material, but talk to them and be a friend.

The other two hours in the middle of the day are for those dealing with global environments. This is key to a better understanding and a diverse view of the community itself.

Communicate with your community outside of SDN/BPX (e.g., Twitter). Get involved in the back channels – give hints of what we are planning, be honest about what is going on, and get involved in the discussion. Look for BarCamps and local meet-ups – make your own meet-up; bring the community together but not in a formal way – have fun.

- Be sure your community knows you are real and you support them and are not just doing a job. Let them know you care (e.g., I send out around 400 e-cards for birthdays a year to the community).

- Call and chat with them; stop by desks and say hi. When I do this, I don't talk contributions, I just talk. I don't pester people to do more. I make them feel as though they are a valuable part of the community. That alone gets them to do more. Once they feel as though they are „part of it," they do what they can to make their part better.

- Blog regularly about something in your area – real content, not just news or an update, so your community knows you have a clue about what they are doing by doing it yourself!

- Use your words and experiences (even if you relate it to a non-techie/enterprisey type, for example). Be open and encourage by leading by example.

- You can't be an evangelist for a specific topic without having intimate knowledge of that area.

- Talk to the rest of the team – use your strengths to your advantage and eliminate your weaknesses with the help of your team.

- Use them to help you find someone who has knowledge you lack.

- Encourage others to be your evangelist. Support them!

Here's an example: I'm asked to be the evangelist for the XI area, but I have to say „no." I can be an evangelist for the XI community, but not the topic. For that I need an XI evangelist willing to take the time and help me to help them grow their community. Help comes quicker than you can imagine!

Through regular interaction with the community, it will become clear to focus the primary efforts on the top 1 percent of the community to enable them to focus on the top 10 percent, and for them, in turn, to be able to focus on the larger community. The community-building ‚formula' used by many organizations works like this: 1 will bring you 9, and 9 will bring you 99. By maintaining a focus on that top 1 percent and providing them with the tools and support, they will help to grow the community more than a single Community Evangelist can achieve alone.

SDN and BPX track these numbers as well as many others, but for the Community Evangelists these are the true indicators of progress and success.

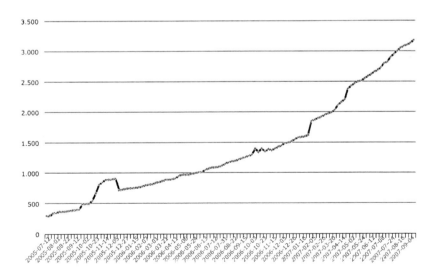

Figure 1: Active growth of SDN

Talking numbers

All social media projects require milestone measurement. Otherwise, you have no idea whether the project is achieving success. That often means looking at the raw basic numbers, e.g., members, posts, visits, etc. This begs the question of how do you verify community involvement based on those numbers? Personally I use the "thank you" method at the end of each day. This simple method only requires that I count the number of complaints compared to the "thank you" notes I receive in any given day. Even though it is a perfectly acceptable measure, the "thank you" method is a hard management sell. It's even harder when thinking about management's traditional views regarding accountability and resource planning. At some point you must revert back to hard numbers:

- Number of members

- Number of logins

- Number of concurrent users

- Numbers of page views

These, I think, are the four most important measures when tracking community and effectiveness across various activities.

Building community requires people, so you certainly want to measure member numbers. There's no point in having members if they are inactive, so again, you want to check how often they log in. At the same time, you need to know the extent to which the community is being used, so this time, you need concurrent users. You need to watch page views to understand what the community members find interesting. Armed with these simple measures, it is possible to start understanding how the community is growing (or not), how intense the engagement is, and the areas of interest that are attracting attention and those that are not.

Dealing with problems

As a global community of some 950,000 people, the SDN community draws from different cultures, working environments, and personality types. These people are also passionate, and inevitably clashes occur. Dealing with problems that require conflict resolution is never fun and I'm probably the only person on the team that will volunteer to resolve these issues. It's the most miserable job in the world because you just know it is going to be hard to satisfy everyone. But when you are driving a community, it's like nurturing a garden and sometimes weeds need trimming.

I've developed my own method for dealing with the problems:

- Respond to all parties involved with a ,touch' that's commensurate with the severity of the problem.

- Follow up responses quickly, explaining why you intervened.

- Be honest and open, and tell them why you had to intervene.

- Find a solution.

There are no magic tricks, no magic formula. The simple, honest, fair, and fast approach is always the best. Last year, one of our community members felt it would be OK to hack our system. This is what developers do. They love to pick and poke to see if they can punch holes in systems. In this case, it was more of a mild crack at the system, but for many it could have been a frightening experience with the potential to disrupt the entire community.

First response and I will paraphrase: "What you've just done is extremely inappropriate and has put us in a position where we have little choice but to remove your account from our system."

The response: "But I only wanted to show you what was wrong so you could fix it."

My response: "OK, I understand, but listen: there are better ways to go about this sort of thing. Send me all the data and I will get you in touch with our platform team."

The problem this member highlighted is one that exists on every single Web site in the world and is not a security hole as such. The point is that not every problem has to end badly, but rather it's an opportunity to better understand how your community thinks. In this case, as with many others, community members are so eager to ensure the best, they sometimes become over-enthusiastic without realizing the potential risks. It wasn't malicious, just foolish. That user has since become one of our most active and productive members.

Spotlighting the good ones

One of the most rewarding aspects of building community is watching people grow in stature and authority so that they eventually take their place at the front of the pack. As a Community Evangelist, it's my job to drive community but not necessarily lead community. Driving community should be done more so by those who best understand community topic and who are the most passionate. I like to refer to those as Topic Evangelists. My job is to help motivate and support the Topic Evangelist. They in turn support, motivate, and lead the upper 10 percent of the community, who in turn lead the rest.

When starting the community, people resources were thin on the ground. We had very few Topic Evangelists and it became a matter of searching for potential leaders, watching who does what, and how often they do it. That has to be done daily and requires an eye to detail alongside the ability to spot trends. This is how you see who emerges as community leaders through a combination of determination, passion, and desire. It's then necessary to understand the individual's underlying motivations. Finally, it's necessary to sift through to find the ones with the right mix of community and topic knowledge. Assuming they are willing, it will then be their goal to continue the process of motivation.

This is the biggest part of the evangelist's job. To this day I search for, discover, and befriend some of the best people in the software industry. It's a process of constant renewal and growth as fresh topics emerge, but is a process that has some of the greatest rewards. Returning to the gardening metaphor for a moment, I liken our successes to watching different plant types grow from tiny seedlings in bare ground to mature and beautiful flowers that carpet the earth in a kaleidoscope of color. Each in its appropriate place, each thriving.

Stefan Böcking
Vodafone and Enterprise 2.0

Introduction

With 241 million customers, making it the largest mobile phone network in the world, Vodafone employs over 66,000 staff in twenty-five
countries worldwide. Built up from a series of key acquisitions, such
as the acquisition of the Indian mobile phone operator Hutchinson
Essar in 2007, Vodafone is active in a number of different markets, its
strategy being guided by the local subsidiaries with their heterogeneous
company histories, cultures, and technologies.

The tightly-knit, efficient global networking of Vodafone's entire workforce is a basic prerequisite for the company to be successful in leveraging its size and international presence as a competitive advantage. As
well as increasing individual productivity by ensuring all staff members
are efficiently networked, an interaction platform also fosters a coherent corporate identity. Vodafone is not the only corporation with first-
hand experience of the transformation of employees into 'knowledge
workers' – people whose daily work is increasingly characterized by
the creation and utilization of corporate knowledge (Davenport 2005).
Accordingly, the maintenance and structuring of company knowledge
via information systems is becoming a core competency, and one with
key strategic implications.

The discipline of 'knowledge management' has the aim of activating untapped potential for productivity and innovation within a corporation. This approach considers not only explicit knowledge – such as is already codified in available documents – but also implicit knowledge, which exists only informally within employee networks. Both forms of knowledge are then consolidated into a single knowledge store. The importance of informal networks within a company can hardly be overestimated, since a far greater amount of corporate knowledge passes through such networks than through the official company channels (Bryan/Matson/Weiss 2007).

Vodafone has therefore spent the last few years building up a global, centralized platform for communication, information, and collaboration, which will serve as a foundation for further projects designed to boost knowledge management efficiency. One of these projects addresses the question of Web 2.0 technologies and ideas, investigating how these might play a supporting role when implemented within a corporate context. The 'social software' approach in particular may well prove to be an appropriate tactic to adopt when attempting to formalize and codify implicit knowledge (as exchanged in informal employee networks) in such a way that other employees can better understand and access this knowledge. Vodafone's activities in this area, which is referred to generally as 'Enterprise 2.0', will be explored in more detail below.

Starting point

Knowledge workers occupy a wide variety of positions in a modern company. Such employees work with both internal and external applications and sources of information in order to generate business value. In relation to the creation and utilization of information within the enterprise, such knowledge worker activities can be summarized as follows:

- Browsing: navigating within categories and topics, not only aiming to uncover the required data, but also to attain an overview of other information on the same topic or in the same category

- Searching: data searched for is described in a system query to precisely target the retrieval of data on a certain topic – independent of the data's storage location or its specific categorization

- Reading: analysis of incoming messages, together with the completion of appropriate follow-up activities and storage of such messages for later use

- Creating: creation of new information – either through the consolidation and interpretation of previously-accumulated information, or by the formulation of new ideas and theories (innovation)

- Interaction: communication and collaboration with other users via informal networks for the purpose of exchanging experiences and contact data

- Organization: storing and archiving data in a structured way to enable its rapid identification at a later point in time

The central question governing a knowledge worker's productivity is thus: "How can I find the relevant data and expertise I need for my work in the shortest possible time?" Companies implement a variety of information systems in order to ensure efficient and effective support is given to the production of knowledge. As a result, knowledge workers not only have to deal with an ever-increasing flow of data: they are also confronted with an increasingly diverse range of related systems.

System diversity

Modern companies provide their knowledge workers with a range of diverse applications and tools that support communication, information, and collaboration:

- Staff portals support company communication processes and provide centralized access to a variety of applications.

- Team rooms support collaboration and the exchange of information within projects or organizational units (departments). Such systems include not only traditional document-based systems but also Web-based systems that implement wiki techniques.

- The desktop PC and the e-mail inbox are used to archive personal information or copies of other data, and also to structure one's own personal dialogue with other users.

- Synchronous interactive systems let information exchange take place in real time, and are based on communication technologies such as video conferencing, instant messaging, application sharing, or telephone (conferencing) networks.

- Document management systems are also used – primarily for storing information in accordance with guidelines and policies specified in relation to statutory requirements governing record retention and accountability.

- Specialized company applications can range from a simple phone book or cross-company search facility to enterprise resource planning (ERP) systems that store information pertaining to personnel, financial accounting, and bookkeeping.

- External data sources such as knowledge bases, catalogs, and directories are also available via the Internet.

Considered together, all these systems present a two-fold hindrance to the efficient retrieval of information: first, there are often too many applications used to store relevant information in a business context; second, there is no clear policy available as to when a certain piece of data should be stored in which particular system.

Information overflow

While a considerable amount of information is generated by product, customer, and supplier activities, the surge in e-mail and corporate collaboration software usage has caused an exponential increase in data. Around three years ago, Vodafone introduced global team rooms for project management. Today, their number has grown to over 7,000, with total stored data amounting to over four terabytes. The data volume increases steadily at a rate of 8 percent per month. This vast amount of available data combined with a continual increase in the total volume of information makes it increasingly difficult for knowledge workers to find relevant information quickly.

Information redundancy also amplifies growth. In this respect, the "Me"-focused desktop and e-mail model is the chief offender, since it encourages the creation of personal copies of data. This is in stark contrast to the "Us"-focused team room model, which supports the creation of a single document copy that is accessible to all parties. An increase in the volume of data does not imply an increase in the availability of quality data. Thus, the fact that employees have themselves created content via e-mail, blogs, and wikis is not necessarily a guarantee of its quality – even where this content is subjected to peer review and correction by other members of the workforce.

In general, and from the knowledge worker's point of view, information can be described as data that possesses a comprehensible significance and is potentially useful. Depending on the relevance and quality of this data, this information is either perceived as distracting "interference" (irrelevant and obstructive to the search for real information) or as "knowledge" (relevant and applicable information) (Zijlstra 2004).

This information relevance is, however, dynamic and depends on the following factors:

Audience: identical information can have a different meaning and a different value for different people or groups of people.

Context: a person or a group of people may find that the value of the information depends on their current situation and set of tasks.

Time: the importance of the information – even for the exact same audience – may change in relation to the point in time when the information is viewed (i.e., how old it is).

This dynamic element in informational relevance makes it a real challenge to supply the required information as part of a company search result. In addition to relevance, the quality of the information is also of importance to knowledge workers. This quality depends on a number of factors, including the reputation of authors and reviewers involved, the validity of the content backed up by verifiable facts and references, and the precise and comprehensible presentation of the information. The iterative processing of information serves to update it and to improve its quality. Within a company, authors and reviewers usually represent a specialist department that has a certain authority in its area, guaranteeing a high standard of quality. However, the collaborative creation and iterative improvement of information that acts across organizational boundaries can also produce high-quality contributions, as shown by studies that consider Wikipedia in this light (Anderson 2006). All in all, it is the sheer mass of available data that hinders knowledge workers in their search for relevant information of an acceptably high quality.

The following analysis discusses the new Web 2.0 technologies and models, focusing particularly on their translation into a business context in adherence to the Enterprise 2.0 principle. So implemented, these tools are ultimately intended to improve knowledge management and thus support a more efficient and more effective search for knowledge within the enterprise.

Enterprise 2.0

Innovation in company-internal interactive platforms has been driven primarily by the Internet. Based on early Internet services and protocols, including e-mail, newsgroups and file transfer systems, the initial wave of online innovation (Web 1.0) brought with it the first technologies and models such as hypertext systems, Web browsers, portals, and open source software – all of which rapidly found their place in company-internal applications and systems. The term 'Web 2.0' summarizes a variety of Internet innovations and trends occurring as part of the second wave of innovation (O'Reilly 2005):

- New techniques to combine (mashup) new services (Web services) in a lightweight manner and improve the usability of Web applications (rich applications) – including drag and drop models taken from the field of desktop applications (AJAX, REST) plus the signaling of content updates to users (RSS).

- New kinds of applications, summarized under the catchall term of 'social software,' support a number of functions, including blogging (blogger.com), social bookmarking (del.icio.us), collaborative authoring (wikipedia.org), content aggregation (netvibes.com), collaborative editing (writely.com), social music (last. fm), collaborative content rating (digg.com), social community (flickr. com), social networks (facebook.com), etc.

- New functions for Web applications such as comment functions, trackbacks, permalinks, blogrolls, pings, and tag clouds.

- New forms of communication integrated into Web applications that depend on the collaboration and self-presentation of those using them.

- New business models based on the theory expounded by Chris Anderson in his book "The Long Tail" (2006), according to which Internet suppliers can turn a profit by selling niche products in large numbers.

- New models for software provisioning, such as software as a service (SaaS), whereby Web applications are offered as a service on the Internet, with the provider assuming responsibility for the system administration and maintenance of the system. An example in the area of customer relationship management (CRM) software is salesforce.com. By 2009, approximately 10 percent of the market for corporate software is expected to be in the form of Web applications (Dubey / Wagle 2007).

- New IT architectures for easy-to-manage development processes and the operation of Web applications. The applications involved undergo constant change: the time frame between versions is a matter of hours, they are subjected to continual improvement via interaction with their customers, and they are always intended to be treated as pre-launch versions ('perpetual beta'). Dynamic scripting languages, agile development techniques that keep the customer actively involved in the iterative software creation process, and an operational model that is optimized for Web technologies are all critical when providing competitive Web applications.

Each of these new aspects has a corresponding effect in an enterprise context. Social software, with its new kinds of applications and paradigms (Richter / Koch 2007), is of special interest with regard to the improvement of knowledge management and search. Accordingly, we will now turn to focus on the transference of social software concepts into the enterprise environment. We may use the following Enterprise 2.0 model as our guide:

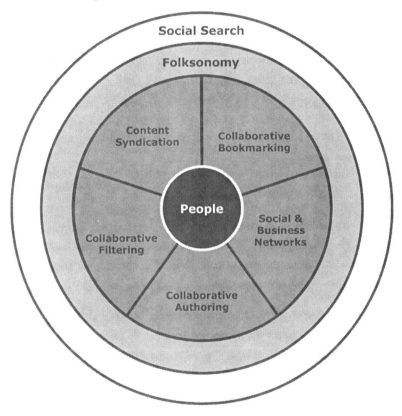

Figure 1: Enterprise 2.0 model

- Participation (staff involvement): Company knowledge is generated and organized by all staff acting in concert. Employees decide which information and which networks are relevant for their work. By creating and maintaining the information as a joint effort, the quality of the information is monitored and successively improved (Bughin 2007).

- Collaborative tagging, folksonomy (mutual allocation of keywords): operating without a dedicated editing team, all members of staff classify the available corpus of company information themselves. The result is a tag directory created by the staff acting in concert: a directory that is understood and supported by the entire workforce.

- Collaborative bookmarking (shared bookmarks): instead of adopting the traditional approach of sorting specialist knowledge into dedicated knowledge bases, members of staff exchange their personal knowledge relating to the company, to work themes and project topics via bookmarks, which link to interesting items of information. The hypothesis here is that the personal collection of bookmarks effectively replicates the majority of knowledge available to staff.

- Collaborative authoring (shared editing and publication): staff are able to work together on the authoring of information or its subsequent improvement in an uncomplicated, ad-hoc fashion. With the possibility of optimizing other published materials as they see fit, staff can thus hypothetically make a permanent contribution to the quality of company knowledge in the long-term.

- Social networking (maintenance/exchange of contacts and networks): the formal inclusion of informal networks and personal contacts enables all employees to profit from these networks, since the process of tracking down specific colleagues possessing certain abilities and experience thereby becomes both easier and faster.

- Content syndication (multiple re-use of content): instead of communication initiated by a third party (push), staff members decide themselves (pull) when to access useful content updates, messages, and changes that occur to performance indicators in individual fields of interest. By channeling these various data flows into a single application (typically, a "feed reader"), staff members can inform themselves in a timely and targeted fashion about any topic of interest.

- Collaborative filtering (mutual content filtering): a technique probably best-known from its implementation at Amazon, collaborative filtering involves the analysis of group behavioral patterns in order to make specific recommendations to individuals whose interests follow a similar pattern. A company-internal application not only displays a piece of information, but also displays links to (i.e., recommends) other information that staff members have chosen to classify in a similar fashion.

- Social search (group search): a company search application that not only searches a standard indexed directory of information, but also considers ratings made by staff as an additional criterion when calculating the relevance of the information before displaying it.

The Enterprise 2.0 model described above forms the basis of Vodafone's own E2.0 program. We will now turn to discuss the latter in some detail, focusing our attention on a prototype for knowledge management and search.

Vodafone Vision – Vodafone social networking

Let us reconsider for a moment the central issue for knowledge workers: how can they find relevant knowledge both efficiently and effectively? Early attempts to provide a sufficiently complete answer to this question had already been attempted before the Web 2.0 watershed, via company search engines and knowledge management systems. However, such systems enjoyed only limited success.

While company search engines can be extended into the area of knowledge search with a certain amount of effort, it is not long before they run up against employee data protection legislation – such as in the area of automatic rating of e-mail conversations in order to deduce expertise, for example. Other problems include the undifferentiated indexing of all available data or insufficient keyword utilization (where limited only to an editing team) – both of which seem to work to reduce the efficiency of the search process. Traditional knowledge management systems, where staff explicitly input their experiences, best practices, and personal expertise, often achieve success only if this act of contribution is explicitly 'hard-coded' into staff target agreements and also given an appropriate priority level. If not, such systems soon become both outdated and ignored.

Implementation at Vodafone

The primary components of Vodafone's global interaction platform include e-mail, synchronous interactive services provided by the staff portal, document- and wiki-based team rooms, a document management system, and a company search engine that indexes both employee information and general data. A mobile portal provides access to the staff portal and selected applications while on the road. The underlying infrastructure provides essential services such as single-sign-on and a central staff directory and also ensures global availability.

The first phase of Enterprise 2.0 at Vodafone was completed at the end of 2005 with the introduction of a new global service for collaborative editing and publishing (wiki) and for using Weblogs (blogs).

Today, this service is used by various levels of management as a (Web-based) departmental team room and also as an informal channel for communication (Young 2007). There has as yet been no appreciable changeover from the document-based team rooms in the area of project work. Use of the service is not mandatory, but has instead spread via viral marketing initiatives. Both a disclaimer and an etiquette guide are placed prominently on the site: the subjects they address include the necessity of acting responsibly when publishing information. Figure 2 shows the entry page of this wiki/blog service.

In the second phase of Enterprise 2.0 at Vodafone (currently underway), a number of ideas for improving the organization and provisioning of company knowledge are being considered. Apart from the optimization of the company search (including its extension to cover additional data sources), field trials of a social software prototype with the working title of "Vodafone Vision: Vodafone Social Networking" are also in progress. We will now turn to consider this in greater detail.

Figure 2: Start page of the company-wide wiki/blog service

Knowledge base

The basic principle of Vodafone Vision is that staff will mark data as relevant for their work by actively tagging information, networks, and people. This data, subsequently marked as "knowledge," may be sourced from a variety of internal and external applications and information repositories. The knowledge base so created by Vodafone Vision will therefore present a digest of the existing sum total of internal and external information. Modifications made to staff activities or goals will be mirrored in the knowledge base by corresponding changes in the informational focus. This living knowledge base is thus a real-time indicator of the focus of the company itself. Vodafone Vision not only offers all staff in the company a general knowledge search, but also provides each registered staff member a personal knowledge management system, transforming the employee into an active contributor to company knowledge.

Figure 3: Knowledge search start page

Personal knowledge management

Each staff member has a personal area used to manage the following kinds of information:

• Profile: professional and personal information

• Contacts: social and work-related contacts and networks

• Bookmarks: personal bookmarks

• Pages: personal Web pages, for recording notes/info

• Agents: specialized search agents for saving search queries; users can also opt to receive updates when changes occur in the searched content scope.

Staff decide autonomously which information they will share with other users (Morello / Burton 2006). All items of information are indexed by staff members with the use of topics (tags), meaning that a staff-organized topics directory is created over time that references the entire body of tagged information in the company. The tag words are utilized to form 'topic clouds,' with type size being used to indicate relevance – one factor for relevance being the frequency with which the topic word has been used.

Figure 4: Start page for personal knowledge management

Changes in the type size and the variation in terms shown thus mirror the company's current interests with regard not only to the various projects and programs but also to hot topics applicable to core competencies and staff-related issues. A number of other functions are also available:

- Recommendations: staff can recommend information to one or more colleagues, or even send anonymous recommendations to a group of colleagues who are subscribed to updates for certain topic words.

- Topic worlds: topic worlds present a filtered view for a certain pre-defined subject, i.e., they display only information that corresponds to the specified topic (formalized network or 'community of interest'). Owners of a particular topic world invite their colleagues to join it. Only members are allowed to contribute content to such a world. Anyone who does not have an invitation may only view the content of the topic world. Such a system lets teams working in data centers or call centers set up specialized topic worlds with articles and links to previous cases and resolutions, while it also allows them to learn and profit from the knowledge base of all members, which they can switch over to at any time. Topic worlds thus give informal staff networks a degree of formality, structuring them as spaces where ideas can be discussed, contacts brokered, and opinions exchanged.

• Each individual staff member may also create subscriptions to any form of information, topic, or topic world that he or she so wishes. Update information (via feeds) is received using a suitable reader (feed reader).

Knowledge search

The knowledge search system is an enhanced company search engine that searches through company information indexed from a number of data sources. The enhancement to this system involves the inclusion of additional criteria for establishing the expected relevance of the search results as applicable to the employee conducting the search. These additional criteria include the following:

• staff profiles

• staff contacts

• formal and social networks

• staff-organized topic directories

• staff bookmarks

• external data sources (e.g. Wikipedia)

The knowledge search concerns itself primarily with the knowledge base that results from personal knowledge management as practiced by staff members, using the general internal and external data sources only as a secondary resource. The search is designed to show the knowledge worker simply and clearly how the retrieved information relates to its authors, and also lets searchers identify the staff members that currently utilize this information and the networks that have contributed to its creation.

Vodafone Vision is currently only a prototype and has a long way to go before being implemented as a company-wide tool. Above all, it must of course prove its Web 2.0 capabilities in the fields of knowledge management and search – and, equally importantly, be accepted by the workforce in general. However, our initial tests in small focus groups have highlighted the potential that the bundling of social networks, collaborative bookmarking, and social search, have to bring us a few steps closer to fulfilling the requirements for an efficient and effective search that provides relevant results for both information and people.

Outlook

Although Vodafone Vision is still only a prototype, a number of questions have arisen at this early stage that themselves exceed the scope of the current project, namely:

- How can new employees' knowledge that is stored in external data sources such as facebook.com and del.icio.us be brought across into the company knowledge base?

- What happens to individual employee knowledge when the employee leaves the company? Will there be something like an "alumni" network?

- How will knowledge transfer to successors be managed?

- How would a multilingual knowledge base develop – and what might be the consequences?

Our work so far has shown us that the business implications of Web 2.0 are necessarily different to those experienced in an Internet context. We believe that Web 2.0 technologies and ideas are most certainly capable of improving company-internal interaction platforms. They thus represent a clear win for staff productivity and for knowledge management in general.

WORKS CITED

Anderson, Chris (2006): The Long Tail. Why the Future of Business is Selling Less of More. 1st ed., New York.

Bryan, Lowell L.; Matson, Eric; Weiss, Leigh M. (2007): Harnessing the power of informal employee networks. McKinsey Quarterly, October.

Bughin, Jacques R. (2007): How companies can make the most of user-generated content, McKinsey Quarterly, August.

Davenport, Thomas H. (2005): Thinking for a Living: How to Get Better Performances and Results from Knowledge Workers, Harvard Business School Press.

Dubey, Abhijit; Wagle, Dilip (2007): Delivering software as a service. In: The McKinsey Quarterly Web exclusive [http://tinyurl.com/667puk], May.

Morello, Diane; Burton, Betsy (2004): Future Worker 2015: Extreme Individualization, Gartner Research, March.

O'Reilly, Tim (2005): What is Web 2.0? Tim O'Reilly [http://tinyurl.com/743r5], September 30.

Richter, Alexander; Koch, Michael (2007): Social Software – Status quo und Zukunft. Technical Report No. 2007-01, University of the Federal Armed Forces, Faculty of Information Technology.

Young, G. Oliver (2007): Firms Use Wikis Mostly for Knowledge Management, Forrester Research, July 12.

Zijlstra, Ton (2004): Every Signal Starts Out As Noise [http://www.zylstra.org/blog/archives/001229.html], March 27.

Stephen Johnston
Nokia: Enterprise 2.0 and Mobility

The question of how Enterprise 2.0 and mobility relate to each other has not been much discussed, yet it seems that many of the defining elements of Enterprise 2.0 are a natural fit to the mobile space. For example, Enterprise 2.0 unlocks the value of data (the mobile delivers these in abundance, such as location and communication history) and relies heavily on web syndication (RSS-style feeds and filter feeds work well on the mobile). Further, there is the potential for the mobile to replace the PC as the primary tool for Enterprise2.0, in particular for small businesses and in emerging markets.

All is not rosy however. The mobile industry faces major obstacles in being part of this interesting arena, for example: first, fragmented mobile operating systems, most of which are not built from the ground up to be Web native; second, the default PC-centric approach towards Enterprise 2.0 applications (big screen, keyboard, and sophisticated browser); and third despite some signs[37] to the contrary, still slow progress by the mobile operators to get out of the way of innovation[38] and introduce transparent pricing and proper flat-rate tariffs.

I would propose that the mobile industry needs to focus less on worrying about who gets which share of an ever dwindling consumer pie and instead target a bigger prize – helping companies "go 2.0". And that means a new, open and collaborative approach with a much wider range of partners than the mobile industry normally works with, so that we can figure out how to bake mobility into Enterprise 2.0 from the start.

Mobile – the ugly duckling

Mobile has generally been an ugly duckling of the 2.0 world, but things are changing. Rich, AJAX-based, browser-focused services make high demands on browser functionality – this is challenging for mobiles, even as they continue to improve in functionality. One example, while reading a New York Times piece on how your friends can make you fat[39], you are able to double-click on any word in the story and a definition is given via a Web service – even though the word is not in hypertext. That is a fairly new concept which could pose yet another challenge for mobile, as today's mobile browser user experience is not designed for such double-clicks.

On the other hand, as we can see all around us, the world is going mobile. Will the mobile element of these services be an afterthought, tacked on with limited functionality, or will it be a fundamental part of the experience from the beginning? One of my hypotheses is that we can't just try and shoehorn the PC experience into the smaller, mobile screen. Services designed for a personal, mobile device with a limited screen and keyboard and that can be location- and context-aware should be different from one designed for a PC. By the middle of 2007, there were three billion mobile phone subscriptions globally, and an increasing number of these are data-enabled. As Web-connected mobiles become increasingly ubiquitous, the number of people using their mobile to connect to Web services will rise, leading to greater incentives for Enterprise 2.0 developers to bear mobile users in mind as they create their services.

In order to understand more about how these worlds fit together, I looked back at the Web 2.0 principles Tim O'Reilly wrote in 2005[40] that seem to have weathered the discussion well. Most of them as we can see are relevant to the enterprise space, but what do they mean for mobile? I'll review them individually, and also include commentary on Nokia's experience in this space where relevant.

The Web as a platform

On the consumer side, the Web is now clearly *the* global platform for developers, entrepreneurs, and individuals. Consumer-focused startups now need a fraction of the money they used to in order to get up and running, and scale with relative ease. MySpace, Bebo, and Facebook have brought social networking to the masses – people who neither know nor care that such a term exists. That this trend is going corporate is one of the tenets of Enterprise 2.0. Consumerization of IT is afoot, and consumer-focused tools (IM, VoIP, and social networks) are appearing either neat (19,337 Microsofties on Facebook) or diluted to taste (LinkedIn and other less colourful offerings). However, the fuzzy, beta-nature of many of these services means they're not suited for business critical functions such as the software that runs our big manufacturing plants. Also, it is still hard for Web-based startups to break into the big corporate accounts – you can't yet code a business lunch or round of golf in AJAX. Supporting this, the Forrester survey found that 71 percent of companies would prefer "tools to be offered by a major incumbent vendor like Microsoft or IBM [rather than] smaller specialist firms like Socialtext, NewsGator, MindTouch, and others". So, the Web is not yet as advanced for enterprise offerings as for the consumer side.

As for the mobile industry, let's be honest – we do still have a way to go. Fragmented operating systems, screen sizes, resolutions, and capabilities frustrate development efforts, few entrepreneurs are making real money out of the mobile Internet or seeing large scale service adoption, and few people would choose their operator to provide their social network rather than their fresh-faced, agile Web innovator. However, let's remember that the mobile is a much more recent arrival than the PC, and there are uniquely challenging constraints regarding form factor, UI, and battery life, etc. It is worth mentioning here that Nokia has been focusing like a laser beam on this topic in recent months – it has dominated recent corporate strategy discussions and is now at the core of our recent reorg and new company structure[41]. Our CEO has said we're now an Internet company on numerous occasions; Symbian is now becoming open and more developer friendly, and our browser is one of the industry's best kept secrets. We're also starting to deliver some rather funky new apps[42], including a mobile Web server[43], real-world browsing[44], and of course the Web_tablet[45] and open-source Linux platform (Maemo). No doubt other mobile players have similar initiatives – as an industry, however, we're still playing catch-up.

Harnessing collective intelligence

Collective intelligence generally comes in two flavours – active dialogue among a large group of people leading to consensus on the way forward, or passive analysis of user behaviour. At Nokia we've embodied two methods using active dialogue – online company-wide "Jams" and the use of wikis for projects.

In May 2007 we held the first of our global company Jams that invited the company to participate in the discussion of our new Internet strategy, and proposal of key action areas. We had active online discussions over three days with nearly 10,000 Nokians, including all the senior management, contributing actively to the formulation of new strategic priorities. As a result the company has now embarked on a new set of internal flagship projects that already have the company buy-in, and has benefited from being able to analyse and dissect the information and insights contributed during the discussion.

Wikis are great at capturing user-created intelligence and are rapidly becoming mainstream in the enterprise space, but if you've ever tried using one of today's wikis from your mobile, you'll appreciate the inherent problems here. Socialtext[46] have been making moves in this regard, but here is a standard chicken-and-egg problem – limited demand resulting in limited development time, begetting limited offerings. UI and synchronization are the key issues to solve. As noted above, services requiring smart and big browsers face an uphill struggle on the mobile. Today's wikis often suggest side-by-side version control review and require a big screen to see the differences. Synchronization is a key conceptual challenge with mobile, since they generally are not "always on". Wikis rely on having one version of the truth – two people making changes to the same item when offline then syncing later is an existential challenge worthy of Schrödinger himself.

Today many project managers at Nokia will generally create an empty wiki space as they start a new project and let the structure and content emerge organically. This example is being played out across the corporate landscape, and could well disrupt collaboration applications that are built on the assumption that the designers – cut off from the action – know what's right for each project. Here Nokia's interests are well aligned with the wiki companies and Web services companies in general – do away with the need for a PC and keep the smarts in the cloud. Once bottom up "architectures of participation" are in place, powerful learnings can then be harnessed – enterprise-focused social networking tools (Ryze, Tribe, LinkedIn) are able to unearth links, activities, and dependencies around the organization which traditional hierarchies and organizational structures miss.

Regarding passive behavioural analysis, the mobile sector is not as far advanced as the consumer Internet services space. Amazon is often held up as the first example of a service provider that lets users benefit from collective intelligence through their collaborative filtering engine. So, why would this not also work in areas other than books? For example, "intelligent" CRM software could scan the salesperson's customer responses and suggest appropriate product offerings based on large numbers of other interactions, potentially also outside the company. Most sales people are inherently mobile, and providing lightweight, usable tools that expose this collective intelligence at the right time and in the right context could be a very valuable offering to mobile users.

There are plenty of ways that mobiles could be used as both in-the-field data gatherers, providing relevant context, or being the mobile manager's tool of choice for viewing and interacting with the wisdom of the crowds who have gone before.

Data is the next Intel inside

A key element of anything with a 2.0-suffix is about shift of control and content creation to the edges. In all companies there is a lot of valuable data created by employees and customers – most of which is not usefully captured. As the locus of value moves from product to service, capturing and understanding these conversations is becoming a key requirement. These customers and employees at the edge now have the tools, techniques, and – significantly – expectations about their ability to make change happen. Wikis and blogs are now full-to-bursting with valuable first-person thoughts, reflections, and data – some unstructured, others in an array of formats. This data is now the beating heart of today's enterprise, and often a unique repository of insights from the experts in the company. Few senior managers will fully appreciate this resource because it has arrived via the back door.

At Nokia wikis and blogs are now going mainstream. There is still, however, plenty of scope for more social tools in the more business critical areas, such as the sales teams and factory management. However, when you're making upwards of four hundred million phones a year with streamlined and automated supply chains, the human fuzziness inherent in wikis needs to be selectively managed. Also there is room for more innovation on top of the many tools that are available. TiddlyWiki (recently purchased by BT) integrates IP-communication plug-ins to the wiki framework, thereby allowing in-house IT executives to hack together innovative IP and mobile communication experiences, without needing long requirements lists, lead times, operator involvement, or large amounts of money. Radical indeed.

I expect to see companies doing more with wikis and blogs, using them for key product and customer data, with relevant user-level access controls if necessary. At Nokia we are using the open source MediaWiki engine for a Nokia Infopedia to make it easy for people to find and then use the key data about our products, solutions, organizational change initiatives, pricing, strategies, marketing initiatives, etc. Often overlooked is the change of pace that needs to take place when the early adopter tools move mainstream – today's wikis are still too complicated and hard to use, so a top-down campaign to encourage wiki use will fail without adequate thought and resources being given to training and education, as well as experimenting with new simple UI developments such as drag and drop and other concepts that people are already familiar with. Salesforce.com's AppExchange and Jive Software's Clearspace are interesting in this regard. We need to get the balance right between innovation and communication in order to bring all employees along this path.

Customer conversations that happen around our products represent the possibility to collect uniquely valuable data and engage in genuine conversations with the people who buy our products. Currently, as a product company, we don't yet do this on a large scale – just a few pilot initiatives and ad hoc discussions around individuals' blogs[47]. Contrast this to Google – every second their search engine receives primary user data about terms that matter to them, the effect of every change that Google makes to its site can be calibrated immediately, and they can get a sense of the pulse of the world in real time.

Moving from the source of data to the type of data – we are going to be seeing next generation Web services start to be built for a three dimensional world, and one in which context is king. This will massively increase the number and type of data sources available as inputs in the creation of Web services. The scope and type of services that can be built using this data are difficult to imagine, because so much of the Web today is in two dimensions – when you are reading your e-mail client, the e-mail service provider does not know if you are in Sydney or Sidcup.

Data can be defined broadly here – from *active*, user-generated tags (modular and easy to submit, so perfect for mobiles) to *specific* data, captured in the background, such as usage and communication metadata. How easy is it for users of our devices to access their own data – where they've been, who they've talked to, what applications they've used the most, etc.? In short, not easy at all – yet.

Nick Carr highlights a critical piece of the puzzle suggesting that Enterprise 2.0 technologies may have a better chance than other newfangled technologies – they make life easier not harder[48]. In particular, the system gets smarter as people use it normally. "Knowledge is captured, in other words, as it's created, without requiring any additional work." The classic consumer examples here are Last.fm's music recognition and Amazon's collaborative filtering – both services allow your profile to become smarter and more helpful to you over time, if you give it access to what you do. So the incentive to use it increases. A fascinating question to me is to what extent relevant data can automatically be captured from the mobile device that you carry with you twenty-four hours a day, and itself be used as input in new Enterprise 2.0 applications.

It is the different types of data available to creative entrepreneurs that should make the mobile industry sit up and take notice. Location information is one key ingredient that is trapped and lying dormant for want of a ha'penny of innovation. An entrepreneur I spoke to recently said he would have been charged € 0.15 for each call that his application made to the operator to get a location fix from their cell ID, potentially resulting in hundreds of euros worth of cost per day for each user. People like him are now routing round this innovation roadblock and using GPS or a consumer-created information database. Location is just one piece of data, but there are many others on the phone – which people and companies you call the most, who your friends are, who was in Bluetooth range over the past few days. With careful management and consumer-friendly usage, such data could lead to new technicolour applications and services that will make today's Enterprise and Web 2.0 services look black-and-white.

Perpetual beta

The mobile industry has unwittingly delivered plenty of "betas" in the past (WAP, MMS…), but they weren't marketed as such. Instead of overhyped failures, they might have been seen as tentative first steps. But then it would have been hard to justify charging consumers the full price. Few in our industry seem to have recognized that the value of rich, direct feedback from users can far outweigh the minimal revenues that are captured by overpriced and underwhelming services. This requires a change in attitude and a more open conversation with customers. This will in turn require changes in our transparency and "corporate voice". It is not about shipping and forgetting, but about partnering with customers who are trying to maximize the value of their investments. The Web 2.0 software company 37signals does this well – a product-focused blog[49] keeps news of almost-daily upgrades flowing and rapid and personal customer support for paying customers results in a high comfort level and willingness to engage.

The beta mindset is coming to mobile: recent examples include Orange's coding camp[50] in August 2007 for developers in San Francisco (which perhaps included some marketing element to boost the launch of their Bubbletop Web/widget service) and Vodafone R&D labs' Betavine which aims to "encourage collaboration in the area of mobile and Internet communications". At Nokia, we've launched Nokia BetaLabs for the public, and internally we have a service called AlphaLabs, which now has over one hundred applications and services for employees to test and provide feedback on. However, it is more challenging to be a tester on the mobile – installation is harder (although our download client and PC suite product are about the most usable in the mobile industry), user numbers are lower so there's less feedback, and there's always a danger that we'll put off our users who download data-intensive applications without a flat-rate data plan. Another challenge here is the current community forum experience on mobiles – it's fairly poor, and most examples are just Web-based forums squeezed to a small screen.

The more interesting issues relate to the topics that today's beta aspects can't handle well; here, mobile connectivity makes continuous feedback possible, and smart contextual awareness means that feedback can more easily be provided automatically. As mobile platforms mature and become more integrated with the Web, expect to see greater use of the mobile as both a direct channel for feedback on mobile services and a feedback tool integrated with existing Web services (an example could be the integration of music recommendation service Last.fm with the music player on the phone).

Lightweight programming models

New, open Web standards are being deployed across the enterprise in particular to enable richer user experiences (e.g., AJAX), mashups (XML), and syndication of content (RSS). These allow individuals to create personalized feeds based on information that is important to them, but may not have a critical mass in terms of numbers of users, to get a tailored solution built for them. Related to this is the concept of „hackability“ – how to make sure that the individuals (either employees or the customers themselves) have enough control over the system to create their „own-label“ solutions, and then, ideally, share with others and improve for the benefit of the whole ecosystem. The concept of hackability is anathema to the mobile industry, and there are some pretty solid reasons for this: sensitive personal data and the ease of running up large bills being two places to start. So clearly there needs to be some thought given to what is opened up and what is locked down. J2ME for example is broadly compatible but you can't *do* very much with it – such as accessing the calling and connectivity features. The mobile industry doesn't have the luxury to sit on its hands and do nothing in this area - our customers' communication needs are increasingly being met by Internet players who are embracing more social services and greater "hackability" for developers.

The core applications of the phone are one example here. How many fabulously interesting consumer and enterprise applications would be developed - within 24 hours - if Web developers using lightweight protocols such as XML could easily gain access to the phone's contacts, call log, message archive, and calendar?

One test for lightweight programming models will be the extent to which „presence“ becomes mainstream in corporate usage. Still the preserve of the young, IM-reared generation and considered somewhat sceptically by incumbent executives, this is expected to become more mainstream. Blogger Alex Saunders describes what he calls „new presence“[51] offering useful applications such as call management, advertising, and enterprise solutions that are enabled by lightweight, interoperable Web-based standards such as XML. It is unlikely that the pace of innovation in this space will fit within the traditional top-down standards bodies' processes; the mobile needs to allow innovators in to access the data and create new applications and services on top.

So, again, lots of potential *if* the mobile industry embraces these lightweight models. In addition, mobiles would work well with "loosely-coupled" services, such as mashups that tailor and filter data before it reaches you, helping you reduce information overload (one example would be an enterprise proximity social networking app that would display the current status of the accounts of customers you are about to bump into at a conference). Map mashups could show you houses to rent within five hundred yards of where you are now. RSS is also well-suited to mobile – not only does it deliver modular, packaged stories that work well on the small screen (or headset), but a feed reader or podcast client can load up a full day's worth of content using free Wi-Fi.

Software above the level of the device

This issue shares many similarities with the "Web as a platform" principle, and if it is not handled well could represent a great sucking sound of value leaving mobile platforms. There is little point in having just a mobile platform – your services should be available on the mobile, just as they are on your colleague's computer, or your car on the drive home. The mobile industry can no longer make phones that treat the Web as a *place to go*, but needs to make devices that seamlessly extend the services available on the Web, and provide the benefits of physical form.

Tim O'Reilly himself uses the example of the mobile industry's biggest (unused) asset to date, the contacts book, to demonstrate how this will be affected:

„*It's easy to see how Web 2.0 will also remake the address book. A Web 2.0-style address book would treat the local address book on the PC or phone merely as a cache of the contacts you've explicitly asked the system to remember. Meanwhile, a Web-based synchronization agent, Gmail-style, would remember every message sent or received, every e-mail address and every phone number used, and build social networking heuristics to decide which ones to offer up as alternatives when an answer wasn't found in the local cache. Lacking an answer there, the system would query the broader social network.*"[52]

We as Nokia cannot just decide not to lose control of the contacts book – we do not have the luxury of choice. We need to actively ensure that core functions have an Internet strategy including but not limited to:

have the Web as a backup, channel for access, and platform for innovation.

The calendar function is similarly powerful, and there seems to be an opportunity here for a really good cross-device core application suite – seamless syncing of the user's core information across multiple devices and platforms, with a core offering that lives in the cloud. Again we can turn to the Web for lessons in innovation – Zyb, Soocial, Fidgt, Tabber, Anywr, and of course Plaxo are doing fun things with contacts; 30boxes and SyncMyCal making calendars work better; and RememberTheMilk and TaDa for task lists.

Apparently 93 percent of cameraphone photos never leave the phone – clearly because the software so far has *not* been above the level of a single device. This is changing, too – companies such as Sharpcast and Shozu, and of course Nokia's own Twango and Mosh, are intent on making it far easier to move media off the phone and on to the Web.

In addition to core applications and one's media taking to the cloud, the browser is also going agnostic and making the entire PC go virtual. Soonr allows you to access the contents of a remote PC from your mobile browser – something that shifts value away from the PC to the mobile. On the enterprise side, companies such as Zoho, DesktopTwo, and ThinkFree are natural partners to mobile companies that seek to commoditize PCs – turning any of them into your own personal machine is true commoditization. So, again while it is still early days, the potential for mobile is strong – here we should aim to be a central part of an ecosystem in which intelligence lives in the cloud and uses the most appropriate device at the right time to allow the customer to interact with the service.

Rich user experiences

Finally, the concept of user experience is key, and has been the driver of much of the shift towards consumer tools in the workplace. Compare the experience of using Skype with using our internal IM client and you see the point: the first is fun, the other is grey and dull. We need to move beyond grey and give these tools a human face; consistent with our goal of creating "very human technology".

The emerging „Millennials" generation (teenagers to thirty-year-olds) are looking to connect on a personal level with others and are more at ease with a meritocracy of ideas than a hierarchy of job titles. Creating visually appealing and accessible solutions (Second Life job interviews, Skyping the boss, AJAX interfaces on corporate Web sites) is going to be just another part of what it means to be Enterprise 2.0.

What does this principle mean for mobile? Well, as processing speeds, screen resolutions, and speaker qualities increase, there is a natural tendency to make the phone sing, dance, and perform to the nth degree. There's certainly room for that in some consumer experiences, but when it comes to the enterprise space, a rich user experience gives me only what I want at the time I want it, and delivering this is the job of many of the principles above. Del.ico.us is a good example – almost everything on the page is there for a reason, and a click can filter and slice the data in intuitive ways. Efficient functions, no wasted space, no flashing gizmos – perhaps a good starting point for mobile service design?

Summary

Above I've looked at O'Reilly's original principles of Web 2.0 from three perspectives – enterprise, mobility, and Nokia. It's worth noting that these original principles were extended in a more in-depth (commercial) report in „Web 2.0 Principles and Best Practices"[53], which gave a nod to Web 2.0 poster child Chris "Long Tail" Anderson[54], and David "Small Pieces Loosely Joined" Weinberger[55]. Dion Hinchcliffe notes that this report doesn't change the substance of these principles, but does provide more context and affirms the link with Enterprise 2.0 by providing more discussion of the enterprise impact[56].

Looking at it this way, the mobile angle seems to be an Enterprise 2.0 story that is not often told, but one rich in potential. I've picked out a few potential implications for Nokia – and the mobile industry – that fall broadly into two categories – internally focused on improving our transparency, collaboration, and speed, and externally focused, market-orientated solutions, encompassing opportunities for both devices and services/solutions. Now is the time for companies to ensure that their Enterprise 2.0 strategies have mobile as a central element, not an afterthought.

Suw Charman-Anderson
Molly's Secret Diary or the Confessions of a Social Software Convert

Monday, June 11

Oh dear. Remember a few years back, when they installed that huge document management system? Well, it looks like they're at it again. Apparently some big cheese has decided that we need some thing called a wiki. I have no idea what a wiki is, or what it does, but I don't see what's wrong with what we've got already: an enormous intranet no one uses, more software than you can shake a stick at, and enough e-mail to drown a whale. To be honest, they can tell me to use it all they like, but I'm very good at ignoring that sort of thing.

Tuesday, June 12

Despite huffing and puffing and threatening to blow the house down, I have been unable to get out of this so-called wiki training. It's happening next week, although I'm not going with the rest of our team, I'm going with a bunch of other PAs. On the upside, I think Nicholas from sales rather likes me, although it may have been an excess of beer that had him draped all over me in the pub last night, rather than his innate sense of good taste. He is really rather lovely, with greying temples and a salt-and-pepper beard.

Wednesday, June 13

Nicholas wasn't in today. Apparently he has twenty-four-hour flu, but I suspect it's actually a hangover. A young woman – Anita – came round to talk to us about this wiki thing. Except she didn't really talk to us about wikis that much, instead she just asked us what we do. She was quite a nice lass, very friendly. She sat with me as I showed her how I use my computer, and she didn't wince once when I opened my in-box to reveal 50,000 e-mails lurking. IT are always complaining that I exceed my inbox size allowance, but this is years' worth of e-mail and I hate deleting them in case they come in handy one day. I suppose I ought to set up some sort of filing system, but that seems like an awful lot of work. It might be messy this way, but it works okay for me.

Anyway, we talked quite a bit about the sorts of things I do each day, like organising meetings, circulating agendas and minutes, organising business trips for my boss, and sending round reports to the depart-ment. She didn't really say very much; she just let me rattle on, some-times asking questions and sometimes just sitting and watching as I do what I do. I do hope I didn't bore her. I'm not quite sure why she was so interested in such little details. Maybe I missed the e-mail that explained it all. Still, she was a nice girl.

Hope Nicholas is in tomorrow.

Thursday, June 14

Nicholas is in today, but he looks like he's been really ill. Maybe he does have flu after all. I'm staying well clear, just in case he's conta-gious. Haven't heard any more about this wiki business, maybe they've realised it's a bad idea.

Friday, June 15

It's Friday. That's all you need to know.

Wednesday, June 20

I used to really like my old typewriter. There was something really satisfying about the way you could bash the keys, particularly if you were in a bad mood and wanted to take it out on something. It just made a good, solid, dependable sound. You can't do that with computers. For one thing, you'd probably break the keyboard, and even if you didn't break the keyboard, people would be worried that you were going to. Besides, computer keyboards just don't make the right noise.

Julia says she's already been on this wiki training thing, and she says that it is easy, but then she would say that: she only graduated from university a couple of years ago and computers are second nature to her. Anything is easy if you know how, but it's harder for an old fogey like me to get my head round new things. I'm not looking forward to Monday. Maybe I should pop round to Nicholas' desk to see if he's still contagious. Mind you, I'd have to catch the flu on Friday in order to be off sick on Monday, which would mean that I would have to be ill over the weekend. I'm not sure it's really worth it.

Thursday, June 21

Saw Nicholas today. Sadly, he's no longer contagious. But he is still cute. And he seems to like me even without the aid of beer goggles. Miracles will never cease.

Monday, June 25

Training day today. Actually, calling it ‚training‘ is a gross exaggeration. There were three of us there. Anita ran the session, which only lasted about three quarters of an hour, and she explained what a wiki was and how to use it. She told us that a wiki is just a Web page you can edit, but you don't have to download anything or upload anything to change it – you just click a button, type your stuff, and click another button to save it. I can't believe it's that simple. I've been getting my knickers in a twist for a fortnight about this and it turns out to be a piece of cake!

I was there with a couple of other secretaries, Wendy and Chloe, who work in the same department as me. We went through a few things, such as how to organise meeting agendas using a wiki instead of e-mail. It's a good job nobody at work will ever read this diary, because the last thing I want to be seen doing is enthusing about a wiki after I've spent so much time complaining about having to learn to use it. But it's great! I know this sounds like a really small thing, but organising our weekly meetings has always been the most tedious part of my week. You send out e-mails asking for agenda items to everyone in the department who is attending. Then you have to collate all the responses, turn them into a sensible list, and despite the fact that I do the same thing at the same time every week, someone always complains that their item isn't on the agenda. How hard can it be to reply to an e-mail? Okay, so I know I don't always reply to my e-mail as quickly as I should, but they've got no excuse!

All I need to do now is make a new page on the wiki, copy across the action items from last week's meeting, send the URL to everyone who is due to come, and let them fill in the blanks. Then I'll just double-check it before the meeting to make sure that nothing has gone missing, and bingo! All done!

Of course, I'm not going to let anyone at work know how exciting this is. I've spent years building up a reputation as a curmudgeon, and that's not going to change now.

Tuesday, June 26

Oh God, it was so embarrassing! I went to make my first wiki page, and I'd forgotten completely how to do it. It took me ages to pluck up the courage to ask someone, but guess what? It turns out that Nicolas has had wiki training too! How very convenient. He came round to my desk and showed me again how to create a new page and how to make things bold or italic. It's actually not that difficult – I just need to write it down so that I remember. These old brain cells aren't what they used to be.

To be honest, I may find myself forgetting this sort of thing unusually often. At least, unless (until?) Nicolas starts to look suspiciously at me. Then I'll have to find a new excuse to get him round to my desk.

Friday, June 29

I've discovered a new use of the wiki! Friday is Cake Day, and the easiest way of deciding who wants what cake, and who's going to go and get it, is on the wiki. I believe this may be what Anita called „emergent behaviour". I'm sure she would be very proud of me.

Monday, July 2

I made my first agenda today. I sent the URL out to everybody and got half a dozen replies from people saying, „What is this wiki thing?" or, „How do I add an item to the agenda?" I just turned them over to Anita and will let her deal with it. I can barely edit the wiki by myself, let alone teach anyone else how to do it. Mind you, the cheat sheet she e-mailed to us is really helpful, so I've been passing that on to anyone who asks. Anyway, I'm looking forward to the day when everybody knows how to use this thing, so that I don't get all of the e-mails asking what's going on.

Wednesday, July 4

I checked this morning's agenda, having not touched it since Monday, and surprisingly, it's all there. Someone has even formatted it, numbering the agenda items. I suspect that was the boss. Apart from answering the e-mails asking what a wiki was, I haven't had to do anything. I'm going to put the minutes up too, and hopefully people will not only read them, but also correct them. I'm a pretty fast typist, but you can't always catch everything everyone said.

Later...

Wow! For once, ‚Any Other Business‘ wasn't crammed full of people who still had something to say. And not only did everyone read the minutes, they were corrected and signed off before the end of the day. I guess everybody wanted to get it out of the way whilst the meeting was still fresh in their minds. I like this.

Friday, July 6

The cake rota is going well. I may even expand it to include the lovely lads in Nicholas‘ team. Not that I have a hidden agenda, oh no. It's up there on the wiki for everyone to see. Ha ha ha ha. I'm so funny. No, really.

Monday, July 9

Anita came around again, to see how we were getting on. She liked my cake rota. This time she showed me some ‚advanced‘ features, which I was a bit worried about at first. I've only just started to feel comfortable with the basic stuff. She showed me how to add categories to each page, and we discussed page naming conventions and how to retrieve a page that has accidentally been deleted. I'm starting to feel like a pro. Who'd have thought it?

We also looked through my e-mail for other things that I could move over. There's a monthly newsletter that I've been sending out that I think might work better on the wiki. There is also information about the vendors we commonly use that I could put up there, along with stuff like how to get a new pencil, or who to ask in HR for expenses claims forms. These are questions that people seem to ask me all the time, so now I just have to send them to the right page on the wiki instead of typing out the information again and again and again.

Anita also suggested that instead of spending half the meeting updating each other on what's been going on, we should use the wiki to write updates that everyone can read the day before. Then we can use the meeting time to discuss actions that need to be taken, leads that need to be followed, decisions that need to be made. And I'm going to put the action points up there too. Having everything in one place is so much easier than it being scattered across everyone's e-mail.

I have a confession to make. I really was sceptical about this whole wiki business. I remember when they started going on about knowledge management years back, and installed this huge system that they wanted us to put all our documents in. It really was a waste of time and money because it didn't help us get anything done. At the end of the day, you'd have that sinking feeling when you realised that you still had to upload all of your documents, spreadsheets, and presentations, when all you really wanted to do was go home. This wiki is different. I am already getting less e-mail now, and it's a much more convenient way to work. It doesn't work for everything mind you – some documents are too confidential to put on the wiki – but it's useful enough to make it worthwhile learning to use. I still feel like a beginner, but the nice thing is that the people I sit by are now using it too, and if one of us gets stuck, then there's always someone around who can help.

Tuesday, July 10

Okay, so this is where it all starts to go wrong. Every six months, the senior sales managers get together in a lovely little conference centre in the countryside to talk about performance, strategy, and other such arcane magics. Usually this is all organised by e-mail. Good, old-fashioned, trusty e-mail. This time, my boss – who is in charge of it all – decided that it would be better if we used... yes, you've guessed it... the wiki.

Now, I don't have a problem with this at all, because I'm starting to see how useful the wiki is, and anything that saves me time and effort gets my vote. But some of those senior managers think that anything in a browser window must be a waste of time simply because it's in a browser window. (There's a story, possibly apocryphal, that one of them banned their use altogether, despite the fact that our intranet can only be accessed by a browser!)

So, I did everything that I normally do: found a nice hotel with conference rooms, investigated travel arrangements, and typed up the draft agenda. Usually there are presentations, some from the managers, some from external speakers, but my boss wants to do away with those as well – he thinks they're boring, and who am I to argue? He wants to put all the presentations they normally do on the wiki, so that everyone can read up on things ahead of time. Then he wants to brainstorm ideas, again on the wiki, and then to run something called an „open space" session instead of the usual presentations.

We put all of this information together, creating sections on the wiki for the presentations, a page for brainstorming, and all that, but instead of e-mailing it all in a big Word file, I sent the other managers links to the wiki with an invitation to add to their pages and ask questions on the FAQ page. Honestly, you'd think I'd asked them to sacrifice their firstborn, the reaction I got. Obviously Anita hasn't got round to the rest of the company yet, because my phone just didn't stop ringing. I spent a good part of the morning explaining to them what the wiki was and how to use it. I don't mind doing that, really, but it didn't stop there.

One of the more senior sales managers was obviously really offended at being asked to do some real work for a change, and sent me an e-mail denouncing the wiki as a waste of time and declaring that neither he nor his staff would ever use it and that I was to stop using it to organise this awayday. That really wasn't much fun. Of course, the only thing I could do was turn it over to my boss, which felt a little bit like telling tales, but I'm not in the position to argue back to senior management.

It would appear that we were amongst the first to be introduced to the wiki and maybe the boss has bitten off more than he can chew by expecting everyone else to just ‚get' it: it took me long enough to get it, I'm ashamed to say. I'm not quite sure how this is going to pan out.

Wednesday, July 11

Yesterday's fiasco is turning into a bit of a political war. Apparently the manager who is acting like a seven-year-old has had a long-standing dislike for my boss and takes every opportunity he can to get in the way of any project my boss champions. Whilst I would agree that Tim – that's my boss – can get a little overzealous at times, particularly if shiny new toys are involved, he's a good manager, and he knows his stuff.

Tim told me to carry on using the wiki, so I'm doing my best to liaise with the other PAs and their bosses to get everything ready in time, but it seems that our sour apple is doing his best to have the wiki scrapped. It would be a real shame if they did that, but I'm not sure how they are going to convince this guy that it's a good thing. He's being rather intransigent.

Thursday, July 12

I went for a coffee this morning with Sylvia, Mr Sourpuss' PA, and we had a nice little chat. After working with him for years, she knows how to get round him, but even she thinks that he is immovable on this matter. She hasn't had wiki training yet, so I offered to show her around. It really only took ten minutes or so to teach her how to create and edit pages, and I felt proud of myself for remembering how to do everything, given that I'm new to this myself.

Sylvia agreed that the wiki would be useful – it's amazing what a caffé macchiato and a little personal attention can achieve sometimes – but she's still unsure how to demonstrate that to her boss or win him over. In the meantime she's going to act as an intermediary, communicating with him about this awayday only by e-mail, but ensuring that he is represented on the wiki, and that he gets the most up-to-date information without ever having to visit it himself. That's about the best we can do for now, but hopefully it will stop him getting in the way of us doing our jobs. Someone else can have the political argument about whether the wiki is a useful business tool, and good luck to them.

Monday, July 16

It's amazing what a weekend away from political machinations can achieve. Apparently, Mr Sourpuss has softened his view on the wiki. Whilst I wouldn't claim that we've had an outright victory, Sylvia must have worked some real magic on him. Word has reached my ears that he's decided not to try to kill the wiki... for now. Of course, we all know that's a hollow threat anyway – after all, my boss is bigger than Sylvia's boss – but that's politics for you.

Tuesday, July 17

I saw Nicholas today. He's looking as lovely as ever. We talked about the wiki, and I told him about the awayday nightmare, and then about my idea of putting the departmental newsletter on it. He suggested I think about using a blog instead – he said that blogs are better for that sort of thing, especially if that information isn't going to change or need to be updated. It's funny – a few weeks ago, I would have dismissed the idea and said that I wasn't interested in something like a blog, because I always thought that a blog was just a personal diary (and Lord knows I wouldn't like anyone to read this one!). But I'm starting to wonder if maybe he's right. After all, a blog, as Nicholas so eloquently put it, is just a way to publish material – it's no more a diary than an empty notebook is a diary.

I'm starting to think that a blog would be a good idea: it would mean we'd have all our newsletters in one place, people could use comments to discuss the news, and it would be easy to search for back issues that you missed. (You don't want to know how many e-mails I get asking for some obscure bit of content from the newsletter a few months ago, which then takes me forever to dig out and forward on.) Plus it would reduce even more the number of ‚out of office‘ e-mails I get every time I send departmental e-mails.

Of course, I must state for the record that my enthusiasm for learning how to blog has nothing to do with the fact that Nicholas offered to teach me. Obviously it's my desire to be professional, and nothing to do with his lovely blue eyes.

Willms Buhse, Sören Stamer
Summary: Enterprise 2.0 – Companies as Social Networks

"Change is the law of life. And those who look only to the past or present are certain to miss the future." John F. Kennedy

As Götz Hamann suggested in the introduction, this book is an attempt to break free from such models as the traditional division of work as well as an attempt to develop alternative ideas for the knowledge economy.

To live is to learn. This applies to companies as well as people. Indeed, companies must learn in order to survive. That is why the ability to actively effect change is an essential skill for each and every company. And it is one of the key tasks for company management – if not the central one.

The increasingly networked world acts as a driving force for continuous change, and is itself possibly the most significant trend of all. In the last twenty years, it has deeply affected both the global economy and almost all businesses. Who could now imagine banks, industry, or commercial enterprises without their worldwide telephone and cell phone networks, Internet systems, or logistics chains that span the globe?

And still change is constant, and continues to accelerate. It has brought about paradigm shifts in society, and these are now reflected in the management of companies. The paradigm change embraced by successful Internet services has been termed Web 2.0. Centralized systems, where a few write while many read, have been superseded in just a few years. Such models were and are simply inferior to collaborative systems. The printed encyclopedia is vanishing, while Wikipedia is growing by leaps and bounds.

Companies are now discovering the secret of Web 2.0's success for their own core business, whether deliberately or accidentally within a project team – generally internally and often to great effect. Company management also faces its own paradigm shift, since technological developments are opening up new possibilities for modeling organizations and their associated cultures. Long-standing behavioral patterns are open to being questioned and challenged – with success.

But can Enterprise 2.0 also benefit traditional companies? Can its ideas be utilized in more traditional companies, whose organization is more strongly hierarchical? The essays in this book help to answer such questions with an unequivocal "Yes."

No modern company would operate the way Ford did when introducing the Model T. The degree of freedom in the daily management of work or in the choice open to consumers has risen continually across all industries. Who would buy a car today, if offered the option of "any color you want, so long as it is black"?

The same is true of the ideas surrounding Enterprise 2.0. The freedoms granted by social media within companies will not be boundless. As with all social groupings, such freedoms will continue to be determined by the standards and principles established within the corporate culture. And this is exactly where management will find its opportunities and challenges. To what degree can and must one "let go" in order to achieve greater company success and ensure continual progress?

As with any innovation, Enterprise 2.0 naturally brings its own particular set of risks. Skeptics point to substitution effects, whereby concentrating on using the new tools may actually lead to a decrease in productivity. Such considerations thus tend to multiply concerns about ROI. Indeed, return on investment is itself difficult to demonstrate directly. As a result, researchers have adopted the strategy of analyzing case studies. Enterprise 2.0 is an area where companies stand to learn a great deal from each other. This book is intended as a contribution to this learning process. Enterprise 2.0 offers companies three tangible advantages, whose potential must be fully developed:

Improve market orientation

By networking employees with business partners and customers, their collective knowledge can be utilized far more efficiently. Innovations can be more readily identified and implemented. The direct exchange of ideas between network participants fosters an appreciation for the relevance of information throughout the enterprise, and also especially from the customer's point of view.

Work together more efficiently and effectively

The application of Enterprise 2.0 tools brings verifiable increases in efficiency. One example is the avoidance of duplicate work in large corporations – achieved by ensuring that staff can exchange information across the enterprise quickly and easily.

Being able to quickly locate experts or the right contact person also helps staff get up to speed in new subject areas or work out ad hoc solutions to issues more rapidly and more efficiently. Knowledge management is not a case of writing the sum total of corporate knowledge into databases – a decidedly specious goal in the first place – but rather involves bringing people who seek knowledge and people who have that knowledge in contact with one another.

The open and lightweight communication made possible by social software is of great use in helping people to achieve a common view of a shared goal. Goal definition itself improves drastically via the integration of the various stakeholders within the company or team. And, since fewer problems are experienced during communication and consultation, implementation time is also shortened.

Innovate more

As a team or an entire corporation improves its comprehension of relevant topics and its aggregation of differing perspectives, it can provide more space for innovation to flourish. Innovation itself is hard to schedule: it occurs in the interaction between your staff members. Innovations thus generally result from longer-term processes, and not brief moments of inspiration.

The Enterprise 2.0 toolset can significantly accelerate such processes, however. By supporting the rapid intercommunication between large groups, social media markedly boosts innovative vigor. The better the network and the larger the number of weak ties, the greater the likelihood of new solution models appearing.

What then needs to be done to utilize the advantages of Enterprise 2.0 for your organization? Which preconditions must be met in order to be able to leverage the full potential of Enterprise 2.0?

The most important prerequisite is a corporate culture that is marked by trust, and one exemplified by the conduct of both staff and management alike. It is helpful to start off with small projects of a manageable scope. Development proceeds step-by-step. Successful change management is about facilitating successful projects. Company-wide collaboration is not the beginning, but the end result in itself.

It's worth mentioning another key factor for success: tools need have the lowest technical barrier to usage possible. All staff members should be able to get involved without additional training. And it should be fun. If not, then the tools will struggle to gain acceptance.

It's true that, at first glance, Enterprise 2.0 seems to postulate a conflict between self-organization and leadership. On the one hand, a degree of freedom must be granted in order to give self-organization a chance. Yet leadership must also be shown in order to achieve corporate goals quickly and efficiently. The solution to this paradox can be seen every Saturday on the football pitch, and it lies in our concept of leadership. No professional football team would dispense with its trainer. He stands at the edge of the playing field. He marshals the team. He sets the general rules of play. And yet he lets the players loose on the field. Within those four sidelines, the players must organize their attack and defense strategies themselves in order to get the goals.

The same is true within the enterprise. Our experiences have strengthened our belief that within a few years, Enterprise 2.0 will be as much a part of the daily life of corporations as the Internet and the cell phone are today. Social software will be as natural a part of the corporate environment as cell phones and e-mail are for contemporary communication. A corporate "revolution," then? Hardly – *evolution* would be a better word. And the rate of change is faster than is often imagined. An evolution that naturally leads to the extinction of companies that refuse to change.

Dear Reader: isn't it time to start "letting go" in earnest?

Glossary

AJAX

AJAX is an acronym formed from the words "Asynchronous Java-Script and XML." It refers to asynchronous data transmission carried out between a server and a Web browser. AJAX is considered to be a key technology for Web 2.0, since it makes it possible to implement demand-based loading of partial HTML pages or of simple user data. The foundation for such techniques is provided by technologies that have themselves had a long history: JavaScript, HTML, XML, Document Object Model, and others.

Blog

A "blog" (an abbreviated concatenation of "Web log") is a Web site used regularly by one or more authors to post articles on any subject deemed to be of interest to its readers. A blog might be described as a diary, journal, or log book that has been made accessible to a selected readership or the general public. It is often the case that blogs allow comments on their posts from other users, and such users may also decide to cross-link such blog posts with their own. The entirety of all blogs on the Internet is often referred to as "the blogosphere."

Community

As in real life, an online community is a place where users join together to exchange views on certain topics and interest areas. The social dimension of communities is hard to overestimate, since they embody a place where people congregate with their peers in order to openly exchange opinions – and, in many cases, digital content – on a truly vast range of topics. Web 2.0 technologies used by communities include blogs, wikis, and social bookmarking tools.

Knowledge management

Knowledge management sets itself the goal of making an organization's data and information available in an accessible and intelligent way to all members of that organization. A precondition for successful knowledge management is the structured and contextualized processing of this knowledge. Today, Enterprise 2.0 technologies enable the systematic and contextual presentation of knowledge that no longer consists entirely of "pure" data or discrete pieces of information, while also simplifying the development and realization of new projects.

Mashup

The term "mashup" is used to describe the intelligent and lightweight consolidation of data and functions from a range of discrete Web services. One example might be the small ads application on housingmaps.com. This application utilizes the Google Maps service to produce a regional map showing the locations of products and services offered.

Peer-to-peer (P2P)

Peer-to-peer is the term used to describe a network communication technique whereby each network member is a "peer" of the other members. Accordingly, all of the networked systems can both utilize and offer network services and resources simultaneously. The term peer-to-peer is also used in a sociological sense to mean a group of peers whose members exchange and supply information as part of a collaborative process that is not organized on the principle of a central coordinating entity.

RSS

RSS stands for "Really Simply Syndication," which is – as the name states – a content syndication format. Via RSS, Web sites can restructure any or all of their content updates into bite-sized chunks, supplied as a "feed." Users can then either subscribe to this RSS feed, or can simply integrate it into other Web sites. Using a feed reader, users automatically receive any content updates for which they have a subscription. This obviates the need to actually visit the source Web site in order to look for content changes. RSS thus simplifies the monitoring of a large number of sources – especially blogs – where updates are generally infrequent.

Social bookmarking

The term "social bookmarking" is used to refer to the creation of Web bookmarks (i.e., links) as a joint effort by a number of different users, in an intranet or Internet environment. In contrast to browser-based bookmarking, social bookmarking systems let users save and manage their bookmarks online. In addition, these bookmarks can be commented on, rated, and also categorized. Lists of bookmarks can then be subscribed to via RSS feeds – a way of enabling other users to get easy access to material on a wide variety of specialist subjects.

Social software

Social software is a general term referring to applications that support communication, interaction, and collaboration. Social software is the power behind social networks such as the online communities Facebook, MySpace or XING.

Tag

A "tag" refers to a keyword that is attached to content such as blog postings or online video. Tags can be freely chosen and are designed to make it easier to find the content so marked. Multiple tags can then be grouped together as a "tag cloud." This enables content items to be allocated to a variety of topic areas simultaneously. Tagging can thus extend or even replace the hierarchical sorting of content into predefined categories.

TinyURL

A service that accepts a long URL as input, shortening it and saving it for later access. When users then type in the "TinyURL," they are redirected to the original, longer Web address. TinyURLs so generated begin with "http://tinyurl.com/".

Wiki

The word "wiki" is taken from the Hawaiian language, where it means "fast." Hosted on an intranet or the Internet, wikis are Web sites that can not only be read by their users but also modified, expanded, and commented on – all in a manner of seconds. Another characteristic of wikis is their use of internal linking between the individual pages and articles via keywords, enabling their users to make rapid progress when researching related terms or topics. Companies can introduce wikis in order to collect and organize specialist knowledge on a particular topic from multiple users. A wiki is thus an appropriate instrument for knowledge management, since it can consolidate an organization's entire know-how onto a single platform, while making this expertise accessible to all of its members.

The Authors

Stefan Böcking, Dr. Ing. Dr. rer. nat. habil.

Head of Web Services at Vodafone Group Services since 2002. He manages the internal Web applications, Web platforms, and Web infrastructure services for the 66,000 Vodafone employees worldwide. Also included in this scope is Vodafone's global intranet – recognized by Normal-Nielsen in 2006 as one of the Top 10 intranets in existence. Previously, Stefan Böcking held a number of research and marketing positions at Siemens AG. After leaving Siemens, he managed both the development unit and consumer internet services operations at O2. After graduating in computer science, with a postgraduate degree from the Berlin Institute of Technology, he then lectured at Technical University of Munich in Computer Engineering from 1996. During this period he gave a number of lectures and presentations on the subject of Internet technology, while also working as an EU consultant. An author of a number of research papers, Stefan Böcking also published the framework document "Object-Oriented Network Protocols" in 1999.

Willms Buhse, Dr.

Member of the Management Board at CoreMedia AG since November 2003. Prior to this, Willms Buhse spent five years at Bertelsmann AG (Gütersloh, Hamburg, New York), working in the field of technology scouting. During this period, he also co-founded Digital World Services, one of the pioneers in the digital music business. His previous career has included work as a consultant for technology and strategy at Roland Berger & Partner. The author and editor of a number of books, Willms Buhse is also a frequent keynote speaker at conferences on Internet business. After graduating in engineering and economics from the Universities of Hannover and Madrid, he received his doctorate from Technical University of Munich in 2003 for his thesis on "Digital Strategies of Competition in the Music Industry." The incumbent Vice Chair of the Open Mobile Alliance (OMA), Willms Buhse was also a founding member of the Mobile Entertainment Forum (Europe) and is a member of the Recording Academy (Grammy).

Willms Buhse has been called one of the "Top 50 Most Influential People in Mobile Entertainment" worldwide. He discovered his passion for the Internet in 1994 while working as a project manager for the first international Internet-based learning project at the University of Hannover.

Suw Charman-Anderson

One of the leading experts in social software, Suw Charman-Anderson focuses on the use of blogs and wikis in a business environment. She consults for companies worldwide, with clients in the technology, finance, and PR sectors. After a brief career as a freelance music journalist in the late 90s, she switched to Web design and project management, designing and producing Web sites and intranets for companies such as PriceWaterhouseCoopers und Hutchinson3G.

In 2002 she founded an Internet start-up, which she then managed for a further two years. 2002 also saw the start of her personal blog "Chocolate and Vodka" (http://chocolateandvodka.com), and consequently her entry into the global blogging community. Her passion for blogging and the use of other social software tools such as wikis forms the basis of her successful consultancy business.

Suw Charman-Anderson is also a firm believer in digital rights and was one of the original founders of the Open Rights Group in 2005. This group works to intensify the awareness of legal issues in the area of digital media, carrying out supportive campaigns and promoting grass-roots activism on the subject. Together with her partner Kevin Anderson, she contributes articles to the Strange Attractor blog on the subjects of social software, media, publishing, and related topics (http://strange.corante.com).

Craig Cmehil

A natural talent in the field of software development, Craig Cmehil wrote his first software program at the age of eight and registered his first patent a mere four years later. His broad-based expertise includes not only the development of desktop applications but also Web services – from backend integration through to GUI design. His recent work has seen a change in primary focus, now concentrating on the users – the knowledge workers – who work with the tools that he and others have developed. His research investigates the uses to which these applications are put and how their users interact with their coworkers in communities at the local and international level.

Craig Cmehil has been an active community member of the SAP Developer Network (SDN) since its formation in 2003. Since 2005, he has been working as Community Evangelist at SAP AG in Walldorf, Baden-Württemberg. Prior to this, he had also worked as a software engineer and Web applications specialist at the international automotive supplier Hella KGaA Hueck & Co, from 1998 to 2005.

Nicole Dufft

CEO of Berlecon Research GmbH since July 2006, Nicole Dufft has more than ten years' experience in the analysis of IT markets. She was previously a Senior Analyst at Berlecon, responsible for the area of Mobility and Business Communications. Nicole Dufft began her career in 1995 in investment banking. After work as an analyst in the macro- and quantitative research department at Metzler Bank, she then moved into portfolio management at Metzler Investment GmbH. In 1998, as Senior Portfolio Manager, she oversaw the establishment of the US-German joint venture Metzler/Payden, LLC in Los Angeles, California.

A professional economist, she was also awarded a scholarship for the Advanced Studies Program at the Kiel Institute for the World Economy. A regular speaker at conferences and workshops, Nicole Dufft is the author of numerous studies, and her opinion is frequently cited in the IT trade press.

Götz Hamann

Business Editor for the German national weekly *Die ZEIT*. He has been writing since 2000 on the subjects of media, the Internet, lobbyists, and civil society. In 2005 he collaborated with the journalist Cerstin Gammelin on their non-fiction bestseller "Die Strippenzieher. Manager, Minister, Medien – wie Deutschland regiert wird" ("Puppet Masters: Managers, Ministers, Media, and the Balance of Power in Germany").

Stephen Johnston

Senior Manager in the Corporate Strategy Team at Nokia. Since joining the company in 2003, Stephen Johnston has been helping shape Nokia's Internet strategy by identifying future developments and sounding out new business models and innovations. A passionate blogger, he is a Web 2.0 pioneer of long standing, having promoted the introduction of internal blogs and wikis at Nokia to support both teamwork and collaborative innovation techniques. Since 2006, he has been managing the company-wide innovation initiative "Bottom-Up Internet," which aims to pave the way for Nokia's entry into the consumer market for Internet services.

Before joining Nokia, Stephen Johnston worked in Brussels in trade and e-commerce policy and has also been an e-government consultant for Siebel Systems. A Cambridge graduate in Economic Science, he also has an MBA from Harvard Business School, which he attended on a Fulbright scholarship. Stephen Johnston lives in London and blogs at http://3dpeople.blogspot.com.

Michael Koch, Prof. Dr.

Head of the Research Group on Cooperative Systems and Professor of Cooperative System Programming at the Faculty of Information Technology, University of the Federal Armed Forces, Munich. After completing his studies in computer science at Technical University of Munich, Michael Koch received his doctorate in 2003 for his thesis "Systems Supporting Communities – Architecture and Interoperability." He subsequently held deputy professorships at the universities of Bremen and Dortmund. His work focuses on collaborative applications and systems for promoting community building/groupware, as well as researching future trends and developments in the area of applied information science. Recent publications include "Social Software: Status quo und Trends" (2007) and "Enterprise 2.0 – Planung, Einführung und erfolgreicher Einsatz von Social Software im Unternehmen" ("Success with Enterprise 2.0: Planning, Introducing, and Implementing Social Software in the Enterprise") (2008). Memberships: German Computing Society (Gesellschaft für Informatik, GI - Special Interest Group CSCW), ACM (Special Interest Group SIG-GROUP, SIGCHI), IEEE CS.

Andrew McAfee, Prof.

Associate Professor at the faculty of Technology and Operations Management at Harvard Business School (HBS) since 1998. His research investigates the ways in which managers can most effectively select, implement, and use information technology to achieve their business goals. Andrew McAfee was the recipient of a US Department of Energy Integrated Manufacturing Fellowship for his doctoral research, which focused on the performance impact of enterprise information technologies such as SAP R/3. One of his research areas is the exploration of how Web 2.0 technologies can be used within the enterprise. He also studies the question of at what point certain kinds of information technology can result in an increased utilization of market forces for cooperative activities. He also initiated the first blog at Harvard Business School, writing about the impact of information technology on businesses and their leaders.

Andrew McAfee teaches the "Managing in the Information Age" MBA course at Harvard Business School. He also teaches Executive Education courses for senior management, including Delivering Information Services, the Owner/President Manager Program, the General Manager Program, and Senior Executive Program from the Middle East. Prior to coming to HBS, he worked as a consultant in operations management, advising clients in a range of industries including aerospace, consumer electronics, white goods, and OEM electronics.

Kathrin M. Möslein, Prof. Dr.

Kathrin Möslein holds the Chair for Information Systems I – Innovation & Value Creation at the Friedrich-Alexander-University (FAU) Erlangen-Nuremberg. She is also the current Head of the Economics Department. A member of the directorial team of the Center for Leading Innovation and Cooperation (CLIC) at the Leipzig Graduate School of Management, Kathrin Möslein is also an Associate of the UK's Advanced Institute of Management Research (AIM) and a member of the Advisory Board of the Peter Pribilla Foundation at the Technical University of Munich. Her teaching work examines questions of interactive value creation, designing for innovation, and the development and utilization of systems for innovation, cooperation, and leadership. Her current research also focuses on these three key areas, investigating how companies and markets use IT to sustain these activities.

A founding member of the European Academy of Management (EURAM), Kathrin Möslein has also served as Vice President of EURAM since 2007. She is also a member of the Executive Committee of the Special Interest Group for Computer-Supported Cooperative Work (CSCW) within the German Computing Society (Gesellschaft für Informatik – GI) and a founding member and representative of the Special Interest Group "Innovation & Knowledge" within the Strategic Management Society (SMS). She is also a member of numerous academic and professional associations in the field of strategic management and information systems. More information about Kathrin Möslein's teaching work and research topics – plus current projects and publications – can be found at http://www.wi1. uni-erlangen.de and http://www.clicresearch.de.

Frank T. Piller, Prof. Dr.

Frank Piller has spent many years researching the design of customer-focused processes for innovation and value creation, the successful management of radical innovation, and the utilization of external knowledge within the innovation process. Chair of Technology and Innovation Management at RWTH Aachen University, Frank Piller is also Co-Director of the Smart Customization Group at the Massachusetts Institute of Technology (MIT), having previously worked in the MIT Sloan School of Management (2004-2007). He received his doctorate from the University of Würzburg for his thesis on mass customization, before lecturing on the topics of open innovation and user innovation at the Technical University of Munich, where he also chaired the "Customer-Driven Value Creation" research group. He is the author of numerous books, case studies, and articles. As an academic partner to the Think Consult management consultancy, Frank Piller helps companies in their efforts to establish customer-focused innovation management, consulting on topics such as open innovation, idea competition, innovation communities, lead-user techniques, mass customization, and product configuration.

His newsletter on mass customization and open innovation is read by more than 6,000 decision-makers and opinion leaders in these fields. His supervisory and advisory board work supports a number of innovative start-ups and initiatives. At TU Munich, Frank Piller was voted the "Tutor of the Year" in 2006 by his executive MBA students.

Ralf Reichwald, Prof. Dr. Prof. h.c. Dr. h.c.

Head of the Institute for Information, Organization and Management within the Faculty of Economics at the Technical University of Munich since 1990. From 1991 to 1993, Ralf Reichwald was also the founding dean of the Faculty of Economics at the Technical University Freiberg Bergakadamie in Saxony. Dean of the Faculty of Economics and Social Sciences at TU Munich from 1994 to 1996, he then served as the first dean of the newly-formed Faculty of Economics (est. 2002) at the same university from 2002 to 2005.

Ralf Reichwald received his doctorate in business management from Ludwig-Maximilians-University (LMU) Munich in 1973. In 1975, he was appointed Associate Professor Emeritus at the University of the Federal Armed Forces, Munich. After holding many senior academic positions in economics at a number of universities, Ralf Reichwald was then appointed Head of Department for General Business Administration at the University of the Federal Armed Forces, Munich in 1987. Between 1983 and 1984 he was Visiting Professor at the University of Texas, Austin and at Syracuse University, New York in

1994. He has been a permanent Visiting Professor at the University of Tunis, El Manar since 1999. In 1994 he received an honorary doctorate in economics from the TU Freiberg, and in 2006 he was named an honorary professor of the University of Tunis, El Manar.

Ralf Reichwald is an active member of numerous scientific and business committees. He is a member of the Board of Trustees for the Fraunhofer Institute for Industrial Engineering (IAO) in Stuttgart and the TU Freiberg, the German representative of the European Academy of Management (EURAM), Chair of the Scientific Advisory Board of the Max Planck Institute for the Munich Intellectual Property Law Center (MIPLC), member of the Editorial Board for the *Zeitschrift Führung + Organisation* journal published by Schäffer-Poeschel and Vice President of the German-Tunisian Society. Ralf Reichwald also chaired the Advisory Board for the Federal Ministry of Education and Research's initiatives "Innovation at Work" and "Innovative Services" from 2000 to 2005. Further information on Ralf Reichwald's research topics is available at http://www.prof-reichwald.de/.

Sören Stamer

Sören Stamer has been guiding the development of CoreMedia AG as Co-founder and CEO for over twelve years. In 1996, together with one of his professors and two of his academic colleagues, he took the bold step of forming his own company immediately after finishing university. From the beginning, innovative solutions for adding value to information have formed the software company's focus. Under his leadership, the company has developed into a leader in the field of people-centric software. Sören Stamer has managed to ensure the continual success of CoreMedia AG, overcoming crises and industry "bubbles" with equal aplomb. In the process, the central tenet of "sustainability and growth via perpetual innovation" has been the mainstay of his entrepreneurial strategy. In the last three years, Sören Stamer has completed the transformation of CoreMedia into a modern Enterprise 2.0 company. Through the systematic utilization of self-organization, the company has seen a sharp increase in its capacity for rapid innovation. The interplay of social software and a receptive corporate culture has also been a crucial factor in developing CoreMedia's strengths in innovation, agility, reaction time, and market orientation. In his blog at http://blog.coremedia.com, Sören Stamer contributes regular updates on staff management in an Enterprise 2.0, the future of content business and social network theory.

Don Tapscott

CEO of the international think-tank nGenera (formerly New Paradigm), which has been delivering ground-breaking research results on the interplay of technology, productivity, business design, efficiency, and competitive ability since its formation in 1993. Supported by funding from thirty global corporations, Don Tapscott concluded the "IT and Competitive Advantage" research study in 2006. This project, which took two years and a total of US$ 8 million to complete, examined how firms are expected to innovate in the twenty-first century. A new project – "The Net Generation Strategic Investigation" – has been underway since 2007, examining the influence of the "net generation" on society as a whole.

Don Tapscott is a best-selling author in his field, his writings concentrating on the intersection of information technology, business, and society. Key publications include: "Paradigm Shift" (1992, with Art Caston), "Growing Up Digital: The Rise of the Net Generation" (1997), and "The Naked Corporation" (2003). His latest book, "Wikinomics: How Mass Collaboration Changes Everything" (2007, translated into over twenty languages), is co-authored with Anthony Williams.

Don Tapscott is also an Associate Professor Emeritus of the Joseph L. Rotman School of Management at the University of Toronto. He has been the recipient of no fewer than two honorary doctorates in law.

David Weinberger

Began his career in the late 70s as a lecturer in philosophy at New Jersey's Stockton State College. During this period he was also working as a freelance author, writing not only scientific articles but also humorous compositions for the *New York Times, Harvard Business Review, the Smithsonian, Alfred Hitchcock's Mystery Magazine,* and *TV Guide.* In 1985, after the college did not renew his contract, David Weinberger moved on to concentrate on strategic and evident marketing.

His "one-man consultancy firm," founded in 1994, achieved success in the US in just a few years, providing consultancy services to clients such as RR Donnelley, Intuit, Sun Microsystems, Esther Dyson's Release 1.0, and CSC Index.

Since 1995, David Weinberger has also been involved in the management of start-ups for intranet solutions, Web search engines, and Web-based collaborative software. He is also a co-author of the best-selling "Cluetrain Manifesto," published in 2000 by Perseus Books. Similar success greeted the arrival of his "Small Pieces Loosely Joined," published in 2002 to critical acclaim in the trade press. Currently, David Weinberger confesses to writing "too much," which includes blog postings and articles for *Wired, Salon, USA TODAY, Release 2.0* (*Esther Dyson's Release 1.0)*, and many other publications. His book "Everything is Miscellaneous: The Power of the New Digital Disorder" was published by Times Books in May 2007.

David Weinberger is also a Fellow of the Berkman Center for Internet and Society, Harvard School of Law.

(Endnotes)

1   http://en.wikipedia.org/wiki/Computer-mediated_communication

2   http://en.wikipedia.org/wiki/Online_communities

3   Translation of original German quote: "Diese Überlegenheit des berufsmäßig Wissenden sucht jede Bürokratie noch durch das Mittel der Geheimhaltung ihrer Kenntnisse und Absichten zu steigern. [...] ein schlecht informiertes und daher machtloses Parlament ist der Bürokratie naturgemäß willkommener, - soweit jene Unwissenheit irgendwie mit ihren eigenen Interessen verträglich ist." Weber 1922, S. 572

4   Architecture is Politics (and Politics is Architecture), http://blog. kapor.com/?p=29, posted April 23, 2006.

5   Ross Mayfield's Weblog: http://ross.typepad.com/

6   http://sloanreview.mit.edu/smr/issue/2003/winter/11/

7   www.claytonchristensen.com

8   Following the announcement that the print edition will be stopped, sales suddenly went up. The online encyclopaedia will now be postponed in favor of the print edition. http://tinyurl.com/34uxj7

9   Natural landscape and recreation area between Hamburg, Hanover and Bremen

10   See the article by Andrew McAfee in this volume.

11   "Breakthrough Ideas of 2007," *Harvard Business Review*, February 2007.

12   http://continuouspartialattention.jot.com/WikiHome.

13   We use the term 'customer' to mean the recipient and more specifically the user of a good. A 'company' is the provider and more specifically the

creator of a good. A customer and/or user may also be a company (in a B-to-B relationship). The good may be either a physical product or a service.

14   For a detailed presentation, see http://tinyurl.com/ptbyy.

15   Zeroprestige.org was an experiment in open source hardware at the Massachusetts Institute of Technology (MIT). MIT shut the server down but the best bits are still there.

16   See also http://msdn.microsoft.com/en-us/isv/bb190446.aspx.

17   Interview with Professor Charles Smith, Chair of the Sociology Department at Queens College, City University of New York (CUNY), December 4, 1998.

18   www.twitter.com.

19   I do not want to go further into Marketing 2.0 at this juncture; recommended literature on the subject includes Torsten Schwarz, Gabriele Braun (Hg.) (2006): Leitfaden Integrierte Kommunikation. Wie Web 2.0 das Marketing revolutioniert. 1. Auflage, Absolit Verlag, Waghäusel.

20   Enterprise 2.0 in Deutschland, Verbreitung, Chancen und Herausforderungen, Berlecon Research November 2007 – Nicole Dufft's article in this volume presents a thorough review of the results of this study.

21   Weinberger, David; Levine, Rick; Locke, Christopher; Searls, Doc (2000): The Cluetrain Manifesto: The End of Business as Usual. Cambridge MA.

22   A riveting account of the Kryptonite case from the year 2004 is given at http://tinyurl.com/34tybd.

23   Gottlieb Duttweiler Institut GDI 2007. Vertrauen 2.0

24   http://blogs.sun.com/jonathan/.

25   http://fastlane.gmblogs.com/archives/bob_lutz/.

26   Rickens, Christian (2007): Klicken statt Glotzen. In: Manager Magazin, Jan 1, 2007. www.manager-magazin.de.

27   www.schweppes.de.

28   www.frost-blog.de.

29   http://direct2dell.com/one2one/archive/category/1022.aspx.

30   Mark Granovetter: The Strength of Weak Ties (2007). See also the article by Andrew McAfee in this volume.

31   Newbold, D. L.; Azua, M. C. (2007): A model for CIO-led innovation. In: IBM Systems Journal, 46 (4). http://www.research.ibm.com/journal/sj/464/newbold.html.

32   http://www.hpl.hp.com/research/idl/people/huberman/.

33   An exciting field of investigation is the question of how the degree of networking present in the company exerts an influence on word-of-mouth marketing.

34   Free paraphrase of Don Tapscott and David Ticoll (2005): The Naked Corporation: How the Age of Transparency Will Revolutionize Business. Free Press, October 2005.

35   According to the definition of the German Federal Ministry of Education and Research, this includes companies in knowledge-intensive processing and manufacturing industries such as the chemical industry, mechanical engineering and vehicle construction, TV and communications technology, plus knowledge-intensive commercial services such as financial services, research and development, healthcare, cultural activities, sports, and entertainment.

36   The survey was carried out on behalf of Berlecon Research by the Hamburg PSEPHOS Institute, from September to October 2007.

37   Information Week Blog: Network Operators' Worst Fears Realized: They Will Be Dumb Pipes, Eric Zeman, July 12, 2007, in: http://tinyurl.com/yrvkue.

38   The Register, "Vodafone says VoIP is 'expensive' and 'unsafe'", Bill Ray, June 7, 2007, in: http://tinyurl.com/2kvfb3.

39   New York Times, Online commentary to the article "Birds of a Feather, Obese Together" (3 letters), August 2, 2007, in: http://tinyurl.com/32azsu.

40   Tim O'Reilly, "What Is Web 2.0 – Design Patterns and Business Models for the Next Generation of Software", September 20, 2005, in: http://tinyurl.com/38c8j9.

41   The Register, June 28, 2007, "Nokia restructuring from strength for mobile internet" in: http://tinyurl.com/yuw4zz.

42   Nokia Beta Labs, in: http://www.nokia.com/betalabs.

43   Nokia Research Center, Mobile Web Server, in: http://tinyurl.com/r5jut.

44   Nokia Research Center, Mara, in: http://tinyurl.com/y883yj.

45   Nokia N800, in: http://www.nseries.com/products/n800.

46   Socialtext Inc., Palo Alto, California.

47   Nokia Support Discussion, in: http://discussions.nokia.co.uk/ discussions/.

48   Nick Carr, Rough Type Blog, "Is Web 2.0 enterprise-ready?" April 12, 2006, in: http://tinyurl.com/2h92bu.

49   37signals Product Blog, in: http://productblog.37signals.com/.

50   Orange Coding Camp, in: http://orange-sf.pbwiki.com/ c0dingc4mp.

51   New Presence, in: http://saunderslog.com/new-presence/.

52   Tim O'Reilly, "What is Web 2.0 – Design Patterns and Business Models fort he Next Generation of Software", September 30, 2005, in: http://tinyurl.com/38c8j9.

53   Tim O'Reilly Radar Web 2.0 Principles and Best Practices, John Musser with Tim O'Reilly & the O'Reilly Radar Team, 2006. Download at: http://tinyurl.com/yczyx8.

54   Chris Anderson, The Long Tail: Why the Future of Business Is Selling Less of More, Hyperion, July 2006.

55   David Weinberger, Small Pieces Loosely Joined: A Unified Theory of the Web, Perseus Publishing, 2002.

56   Dion Hinchcliffe, Enterprise Web 2.0, in: http://blogs.zdnet.com/ Hinchcliffe/.